New THE GARDENERS' WORLD HANDBOOK

More Expert Advice from the BBC TV
Gardeners' World Team

Edited by John Kenyon & Phil Franklin

BBC BOOKS

The following gardening books
are also available from BBC Books:

Daytime Live Gardening
First Time Gardening
First Time Planting
Victorian Kitchen Garden
Gardeners' World Gardening for Beginners

Front cover photograph by S & O Mathews
Drawings by Kate Simunek

Published by BBC Books,
a division of BBC Enterprises Limited,
Woodlands, 80 Wood Lane, London W12 0TT
First published 1990

ISBN 0 563 21512 7

Set in 10/11 point Goudy Old Style by
Goodfellow & Egan Ltd, Cambridge
Printed and bound in Great Britain by
Redwood Press Ltd
Cover printed by Richard Clay Ltd, Norwich

◆ Contents ◆

MAKING A
◆ GARDENERS' WORLD ◆
PROGRAMME

by John Kenyon

'How did you find that garden we saw on Friday night?' It's a question often asked, and usually the follow-up is: 'Wasn't that herbaceous border splendid?' or some other reference that is basically complimentary. Alas, occasionally it's: 'Crikey, you were scratching around. You'd have done better in my garden, weeds and all.' Well, we don't win them all – but most, I think.

So how do we choose the gardens we feature in the *Gardeners' World* television programmes and why? I shall attempt to answer these questions by first explaining what we are trying to do. We aim to entertain, to educate (with a very small 'e') and, most important, to encourage you to take a greater interest in your garden and thus get more pleasure from it. Gardening can so easily be regarded as a chore, and yet, once committed to a few small projects, be they raising cabbages from seed or taking some cuttings, most people become at least partially hooked. There is joy to be had without too much effort, even if you've only a tub, a window box and a hanging basket. So we want to spur you into action by indicating what you might try by giving a good outline of what's involved. Television is not, alas, a medium for the total blueprint.

◆ CHOOSING THE GARDENS ◆

Our home garden is Barnsdale, owned and run by Geoff Hamilton. It's quite a new garden – it was a field just six years ago, and it gets better and better as the years pass. So why go anywhere else to make the TV programmes?

There are plenty of good reasons: it enjoys a Midlands climate; there are no salt problems from ocean gales; it has a potentially wonderful soil, and because Geoff lives in the country and has unlimited access to farmyard manure, he has a head start. Another very important reason for going elsewhere is that he is a rather good gardener and we need to see what ordinary mortals do. Most of us who are anxious to learn something want to discover how to deal with our special problems, and there is always someone else who's got them. So in planning a *Gardeners' World* programme year, which we have to do in the preceding November, we're conscious of climate, geography, soil type and, of course, the seasons. We want to go north, south, east and west; we want chalk, peat, clay and sand and, most of all, we want gardeners who are keen, knowledgeable and pleasant with it.

Where do we find them? Well, there is a gardening 'mafia': journalists and PR people working in the field are good sources of ideas and potential locations. Then we have our correspondents. Letters arrive in hundreds saying, 'Why don't you come and make a programme from my garden?' or 'I know someone down the road who has a super garden'. I particularly like the latter type.

So we are not short of choices. What is difficult is to make the right ones.

◆ THE PRESENTERS ◆

We get a number of offers from people wanting to be *Gardeners' World* presenters who think they are God's answer to television, and television gardening in particular. Some may be right, but we can provide work for only four or five, and even then it's very occasional work, not a way to earn a living. There are a great many criteria for a good presenter, but two stand out above all:

1 He or she must be welcome both in the home of a retired colonel living in Cheltenham and in the living room of a miner's widow in Ashington. Television gardeners must have very pleasant personalities.

2 He or she must know his/her stuff. It's easy to teach a gardener enough about television for their authority to be transmitted satisfactorily. However, it's impossible to teach a tv personality about gardening.

Our presenters know their stuff and they are very nice people, hence we get very few adverse criticisms of them. But they are not regular television presenters – they don't get enough practice – so if there is a very occasional pause while they gather themselves, be sympathetic.

In choosing who presents what, it's horses for courses. Roy Lancaster, one of the world's best plantsmen, is wonderful at extolling the virtues of trees, shrubs, herbaceous plants and so on, but his enthusiasm for cabbages is not world renowned. John Kelly is in the same mould, an alpine nutter. Anne Swithinbank likes cabbages and is a real houseplant freak and Geoff Hamilton loves everything! In fact, they all know a good deal about every aspect of gardening, but that extra enthusiasm for their specialities is reflected in the way they tell you about them.

◆ THE TECHNICALITIES ◆

Making television programmes appears incredibly complicated. It isn't, because it's team work. With the help of five or six highly qualified engineers and a couple of good cameramen with some enthusiasm for the programme, the dumbest producer/director can relax and get on with his bit.

The facilities that we normally use for *Gardeners' World* are packed into the equivalent of two smallish furniture vans and we may have a generator as well. One van transports the cameras, cables, enormous numbers of other bits and pieces, and the tea-making equipment. The other van is a technical masterpiece, with two recording machines, vision control, a sound desk. In fact, it's a studio control system on wheels.

Until recently we've had a caption generator for all those ghastly long Latin names of plants, and a slide box through which we could film still pictures, so that the whole outfit was self-contained. You could walk away at the end of the recording with a tape complete and ready for transmission.

All of this adds up to a very big investment, and that's why we have to sort out our schedule for the following year in November. The BBC doesn't have many of these units and it works them hard, so you have to book early if you want one: they are used for programmes on all manner of subjects, including tennis, golf, religion and antiques.

Birmingham, Bristol and London provide these two camera units for *Gardeners' World* recordings, and they are a delight to work with. A small team that achieves a lot in a short time really does get job satisfaction. The gardeners we go to record may be initially a little alarmed by this circus, but they quickly relax because they can feel the friendship between the team members.

◆ PROGRAMME SUBJECTS ◆

There are two irreconcilable aspects to planning what subjects each programme should cover: the theory and the weather. It is perfectly possible, particularly in the case of Barnsdale programmes, to sit down at the beginning of the year and pencil in the contents of every programme from January to October. The lists look impressive, we've often done them, but our climate invariably makes a nonsense of most of the ideas. Forsythia blooms in November, potatoes aren't ready to dig until August. Well, it's not as extreme as that, but anticipating what nature will do requires a very large crystal ball and we haven't got one.

So what do we do? We try to stick to at least one well planned specific subject in each programme, though even that can go wrong. A recent feature on beekeeping had to be postponed for three weeks because on the day of the recording it was so cold that the bees, very sensibly, were not venturing out of the hive. And a frequent problem is that the soil is like porridge, and it would be quite wrong to try to plant anything.

However, for most programmes our special feature and, very often, our expert to embroider it, are the lynch pin, and the rest of the programme content we choose off the seat of our pants. There are always a host of interesting and unanticipated happenings in any garden. Presenters and other contributors all kick in their ideas, and, fortified with this advice, the producer comes up with a running order for the programme: who is doing what and where, and very roughly for how long. To an outsider it might appear to be a very disorganised way of setting about an important task, but if it has the odd weakness, it has a number of strengths.

Topicality is a most important ingredient in *Gardeners' World*. We record on Tuesday/Wednesday for transmission on Friday, and the vagaries of the weather – frost, drought, storm, or whatever – have a vital effect on the sort of advice included in the programme. Pests and diseases may suddenly appear and need immediate attention. Of course, we have belt and braces too. Anne Swithinbank always has a van full of houseplants in case of some disaster. You don't see them very often because there is usually something topical and more important for her to feature. And Geoff Hamilton can always knock up another cold-frame at a moment's notice.

◆ PROGRAMMES FROM OTHER COUNTRIES ◆

We don't do very many programmes abroad, largely because our budget is not very big, though that is not to say that it can't be stretched occasionally. A programme from some other part of the world is not easy to make, for reasons that the average gardener in the UK may not appreciate. The fact is that in these islands we have the most incredible range of plants available to us: the old plant hunters searched out and imported just about every plant in the world that will grow here, so that there is little chance of finding something new elsewhere. Gardens in Italy, Florida, New Zealand and even Japan are growing plants that are either familiar or irrelevant. The irrelevant are exotic and magnificent, but they won't grow in our climate.

◆ DISASTERS ◆

Every recording day presents some unexpected hazard – the zoom on a lens is sticky, the recording machines get too hot, the slides to show those plants in flower are scratched and not in sharp focus, or it rains. Oh, doesn't it rain! As long as there isn't a torrent, we carry on, and the pictures are usually superb. It snows too, but I've only once packed it in and sent the unit home. It didn't make any sense to be digging through a foot of the stuff.

Difficulties don't often compound, but we did have more than our fair share at Sizergh Castle in Cumbria. The Simon Hoist, a very expensive extra ordered to give a birds'-eye view of the garden, sank to its axles in a boggy bit of field, miles away from its proper location. Then one of the recording machines developed a non-repairable fault, followed shortly afterwards by the generator stuttering to stillness. At this point it started to rain – not that misty, Lake District stuff: the heavens opened.

It says a good deal for the perseverance of the Bristol crew that we still staggered on. They ran a cable into the Castle and fired up the equipment from a 13 amp plug. With rain pouring down the camera lenses, we recorded Graham Rose of the *Sunday Times* prancing along the edge of the lake looking like a drowned rat. An unusual sequence, but quite effective.

It was somewhat different in Christchurch, New Zealand. Jean Laughton, Geoff Hamilton and I were about to record a programme in the Botanic Garden, and I was packing my briefcase prior to leaving the hotel. Geoff poked his head round the door of my room.

'You know,' I said, 'the key to the smooth running of any production, especially when you're foreign, is good organisation.'

We set off for the car, but I couldn't unlock the door. It was not surprising: the bedroom key didn't fit. I'd posted the car keys in the foyer of the hotel.

That was soon put to rights and we set off for the garden. As we waited to turn on to the dual carriageway, a passing car blared its horn at us. So far as I could tell, I was committing no offence. All clear and I accelerated away. Twenty yards up the main road, there was a nasty thump behind us. In the mirror I saw my briefcase turning cartwheels and spilling papers everywhere. I'd left it sitting on the car roof!

It took us twenty minutes to gather up the bulk of the papers. This really was a disaster. Sequence notes and the running order for the Christchurch programme were not recovered, neither were the addresses and telephone numbers relevant to the programme in Dunedin that we were due to record the following week. Christchurch is a windy place. I reckon there are still some samples of my good organisation wafting around the city.

SOMETHING DIFFERENT
• OUT OF SEASON •

by Joy Larcom

• THE 'HUNGRY GAP' •

When diehard vegetable growers talk about the 'Hungry Gap', they usually mean the period between February and May, when fresh vegetables are at their scarcest. Everybody's 'Hungry Gap' is a little different: so much depends on how many 'growing days' you have in your part of the country – that is, the number of days between the last frosts of spring and the first frosts of winter. The 'Hungry Gap' is a lot shorter in Cornwall, for example, than it is in the north of Scotland or East Anglia, where I garden.

To me the 'Hungry Gap' is not so much a time when there is *nothing* to pick from the garden as no longer having those scrumptious summer vegetables which no shop can ever match for flavour: home-grown peas and beans; new potatoes; tomatoes with real flavour; beautiful crisp lettuce and so on. Once the summer feast is brought to an end by the frosty nights of autumn, even home-grown vegetables become a little more boring. It's back to basics: brassicas and root crops.

Now I wouldn't be without my hardy Savoys and 'January King', the Brussels sprouts and kale, the parsnips dug from the frozen ground and beets, swedes and turnips prised out of their clamps and sandboxes. It's just that I long for something different – something fresh and green for a winter salad, something with an unusual flavour to tickle the winter palate . . . a little excitement.

Finding 'something different' for the winter months has been a bit of an obsession in my twenty years of vegetable growing, and – casting all modesty aside – I feel I've succeeded in my self-appointed task. As a result I'm almost as busy sowing my winter crops in July, August, September and even October as I am in spring and early summer sowing the traditional vegetables.

I've had two lines of approach. The first has been to track down forgotten and unknown hardy vegetables, which can take their place outside among the Brussels sprouts and kale. The forgotten vegetables are mainly old European salad crops; while the unknown ones have come from the Orient, most of them being brassicas.

9

The second line of approach is to extend the growing season of summer and autumn vegetables by making full use of protection. Nowadays the term 'protection' covers everything from unheated greenhouses (which are so often idle in winter) to small 'walk-in' polythene tunnels, low polythene tunnels, frames, cloches and (the most recent development) light woven film which can be laid over plants to protect them from the cruel winds of winter and spring.

In practice the two approaches overlap, as I grow a number of the more unusual hardy vegetables under cover as well as outside. It's not that they wouldn't survive outside in most winters, but they are more lush and tender when grown under cover, protected from the toughening buffeting which is inescapable outdoors in winter. Tenderness is particularly appreciated with the winter salad crops, where there is no way of disguising toughness by cooking.

♦ THE HARDY GANG ♦

The following, in alphabetical order, are some of the hardy vegetables which I wouldn't be without in winter. In terms of surviving adverse weather most of them are much tougher than they look! Who would believe that the gentle-looking cornsalad (lamb's lettuce) could survive virtually any winter conditions encountered in the British Isles? Or that mange-tout peas are as hardy as the hardy dwarf round-seeded peas some of us sow each autumn (mainly, I suspect, as an act of charity for mice and pigeons)?

Sowing dates for these vegetables vary from spring to early autumn, according to crop. I generally sow in soil blocks or one of the cellular trays, so that nice sturdy plants develop, ready for planting out when a piece of ground is cleared. They can equally be sown in seedboxes, pricked out and transplanted, or, in most cases, sown *in situ* in open ground.

Where this means sowing at the height of summer when the soil is very dry, I invariably use the 'wet drill' method. For this you draw the drill, then soak it, taking care *not* to water the soil on either side of the drill. The seed is then sown in the wet soil, and covered with *dry* soil from beside the drill. This dry soil acts as a mulch, breaking the capillary action in the soil and so preventing the moisture from evaporating from the drill. The seeds then keep moist without any additional watering until well and truly germinated.

Leaf, Green or Cutting Celery

Leaf, green or cutting celery is a rather bushy plant, much closer to wild celery than the trench and self-blanching celeries we normally grow. Whereas ordinary celery is rather neurotic, prone to bolting, fussy about soil, fussy about how it is sown and not reliably hardy, leaf celery is exceptionally easy and remarkably hardy. It is widely grown on the continent, where the leaves and slender stems are used for seasoning, for making soup and, when tender, in salads.

Cultivation For winter use sow from late spring to early summer, either *in situ* or in seedboxes, pricking out and planting outside about 9 inches (22.5 cm) apart. You can also sow or plant several seedlings together in little clumps about 5 inches (12.5 cm) apart, cutting them young, when a few inches high and at their most tender. Most plants can be cut several times.

Once established, leaf celery will sow itself. Just leave a clump to run to seed and you will find plants all over your garden ever afterwards.

Although hardy, plants will die back in severe weather, so it is worth having one or two under cover for use in mid-winter.

Chicories

Several members of the chicory family are useful winter plants. They are closely related to the pretty, blue-flowered, wild chicory which grows on roadsides, especially in chalky areas. Best known here are Belgian or Witloof chicory, grown for its blanched, white chicon (the bud which develops after the leaves have been cut back), and the red Italian chicory, sometimes known by its Italian name *radicchio*, which has become quite the thing in smart restaurants in recent years.

Red Chicory

Most of the red chicories look like unkempt, broad-leaved dandelions with slightly variegated leaves when growing in summer. But once the nights get cooler their leaves turn red and curl inwards (this is said to be a defence against cold), eventually forming a tight heart of pinkish or variegated crispy leaves. These are much sweeter-flavoured then the green outer leaves, which can be sharp-tasting. They are mainly used in salads, though they can be cooked – for example, braised.

They are not completely hardy, but will survive several degrees of frost outside, and more if protected under cloches. It has to be said that not *all* red chicories form these attractive heads. A lot depends on the seed and growing conditions. Some new varieties, which unfortunately have not yet filtered through to amateurs, are a great improvement on the old varieties. In my experience red chicories make much better heads when grown under cover. So try a few in an unheated greenhouse or a frame.

Cultivation The main sowing is in June and July, either *in situ*, thinning to about 10 inches (25 cm) apart, or in seedboxes and transplanting. If you want to try a few under cover, make a late sowing at the end of July or in early August, planting out at the end of August or early September.

11

Treviso Chicory

Treviso is a variety of chicory that doesn't form a heart but has narrow, bladed leaves which develop a deep, glowing red colour in cold weather. It is completely hardy, bringing a wonderful splash of colour into the garden in winter. (I understand it was grown at Kew Gardens last year among daffodils: what a striking colour combination that must have been.)

From the flavour point of view Treviso leaves are a little on the sharp side, though if mixed with other salad leaves and a French dressing they are very palatable. But I must admit I grow it primarily for its garnishing and decorative value. However, like Witloof chicory (see below), plants can be lifted, gently forced and blanched in the dark. This produces exquisite white leaves with pink tips, which are much sweeter, have a lovely crisp texture and look superb in a winter salad.

Cultivation Grow as red chicory above. Allow a few plants to run to seed in spring; they make wonderful spires of reddish-leaved plants, sometimes 6 feet (2 m) in height, covered with pale blue flowers. The flowers, incidentally, can also be used in salads, and have a faint chicory flavour.

Witloof Chicory

A familiar sight in greengrocers and supermarkets, Witloof chicory is very easy to grow and force at home. The variety 'Normato' is one of the best available.

Cultivation Sow from May to early July *in situ* and thinning to 9 inches (22.5 cm) apart. The plants require no attention until November, when they are dug up. Cut the leaves off an inch or so above the stump, reject any very thin roots less than about 1 inch (2.5 cm) in diameter at the top, and store the roots lying flat in a box of sand.

For a household supply it is best to force a few at a time. A simple method is to pack two or three roots closely together in slightly moist soil in a large flower pot, covered with an upturned pot of the same size, with the drainage holes blocked to exclude light. Put the pots into an airing cupboard or somewhere slightly warm – the temperature should be no higher than 55°(13°C) – and within three to four weeks beautiful chicons should have developed. Don't let the soil dry out.

Alternatively, plant them close together under the staging in a greenhouse, devising some method of excluding light. This can be done in many ways. I usually cover the plants with black polythene film laid over steel hoops to make a low tunnel.

The ideal chicon

Claytonia (Winter Purslane)

Claytonia is a dainty salad plant with succulent leaves which have a fresh, pleasant taste: children love it. It is sometimes found naturalised in the wild, though it is not a native. It was originally introduced to the British Isles in the eighteenth century from America, where it was known as miner's lettuce, being one of the wild plants the Californian gold miners gathered as winter greens to prevent scurvy. The first leaves to appear are on short stalks and are triangular in shape. The later leaves are larger, and are wrapped around the flower stalks in a curious way. The whole plant is edible – leaves, stems and the pretty white flowers.

Although claytonia doesn't like very severe winters (it literally goes blue with the cold), it grows very rapidly in autumn and early spring, at a time when salad material is very scarce. It thrives in light soil and seems to tolerate drier conditions than most vegetables, but it also flourishes in my heavy clay soil.

.The Latin name for the edible claytonia is *Claytonia perfoliata*. Beware of *Claytonia sibirica*, which grows wild in various parts of the country. It has beguiling pink flowers, but the leaves have an unpleasant aftertaste.

Cultivation As claytonia seeds are tiny it is probably best to start them in a seedtray and prick out, planting 4–5 inches (10–12.5 cm) apart. You can also broadcast the seed, cutting the plants at the seedling stage when 2–3 inches (5–7.5 cm) high. Allow a few plants to run to seed, and in autumn and spring you will suddenly find claytonia springing up every-where. The seedlings are easily pulled up, so there is no risk of it becoming invasive.

This is another case in which it is worth making a second later sowing towards the end of August, transplanting a few plants under cover in September or early October. The shelter will make them grow very lusciously, and they will be most useful very early in spring, before the outdoor plants have really got into their stride. As with the outdoor plants, if you allow a couple of plants to go to seed they will reappear year after year in your greenhouse or frame.

Corn Salad

Mild-flavoured and mild-looking, corn salad is an old-fashioned, humble little salad plant, a native of the British Isles. It survives the most severe winters, but benefits from the protection of cloches or frames, or even a little bracken laid lightly over the plants in bad weather to keep them in better condition. Although a small plant, it is fairly slow-growing.

Cultivation Make the first sowings in June and July for autumn use, either *in situ*, thinning plants about 4 inches (10 cm) apart each way, or in seedboxes and transplanting. It can also be grown as a cut-and-come-again seedling crop. For this either broadcast the seed or sow it in fairly wide drills (say, 4 inches (10 cm) wide). Cut the seedling when 2–4 inches (5–10 cm) high, leaving the roots to re-sprout. These will be exceptionally tender.

For the main winter crop sow in August and September. These can be grown in the open, or covered with cloches, or transplanted into a greenhouse, polythene tunnel or frame. Either pick a few leaves at a time or harvest the whole plant at once, but don't pull it up as new leaves will often develop.

Like so many old-fashioned salad plants, corn salad will often seed itself if a few plants are allowed to run to seed in spring. The little blue flowers look quite like forget-me-nots. In the past it was sometimes sown in summer between rows of maturing onions, ready to take over after the onions were lifted.

Hamburg Parsley

I always want to beat the drum for Hamburg parsley as it is an excellent dual-purpose winter vegetable, overshadowed by the closely-related parsnip. The shiny, healthy-looking leaves remain green in almost all winters and can be used like parsley, while the root is very much like that of the parsnip. I think it is less knobbly and easier to scrape, besides being easier to grow than ordinary parsnips, tolerating slightly poorer conditions and light shade, and not taking quite so long to mature. The roots, however, are never quite as large as parsnip roots.

Cultivation Sow from March to May *in situ*, thinning plants to about 5 inches (12.5 cm) apart. Treat them like parsnips, leaving them in the soil in winter and lifting as required. Because the leaves remain green there is less of a problem finding the plants in snowy conditions!

Daubenton Kale

I have only recently grown this old, perennial kale, closely related to the wild cabbages which originated on the coasts of western Europe. Like many of the kales it is very hardy, but it is unlike most kales in having very delicately flavoured shoots similar to those of purple sprouting broccoli but a little thinner. It is a prime candidate for the 'vegetable gap'. In my garden during the last two years it has been ready from February onwards, and I've been able to pick it over several weeks. I knew I was on to a good thing with Daubenton kale when I asked my children what vegetable they wanted for supper and they actually *asked* for kale!

In my own garden it was originally grown in the perennial patch behind the rhubarb, alongside the 'Nine Star' perennial broccoli. I have my suspicions about what went on back there: several strange-looking brassicas have appeared . . . bearing a strong resemblance to broccoli but with a touch of kale about them!

Cultivation Sow it any time from late spring to early summer. A few plants would be sufficient for most households. Sow seeds in a small pot, cellular tray, etc., thinning to one seedling per pot, and allow a square yard per plant when planting out. Each will develop into a large, rather sprawly specimen with almost woody branches. The plants last for about 4 or 5 years, each year some of the branches producing flowering shoots and others just continuing to grow. As with purple sprouting broccoli, the shoots should be picked before they flower. If they get ahead of you and start to bolt, cut them back so that the plants don't expend energy in flowering. Where the plants are very vigorous or grown in an exposed position, they may need staking or some kind of support to keep them clear of the ground. Seed is available only from seedsman J. W. Boyce (address on page 21).

Land Cress

Frequently twinned with cornsalad, land cress is a hardy, native plant which remains green throughout most winters. The strong flavour is almost identical to that of water cress, and it is used in the same way, as a salad plant or to make soup, though it is far less succulent than the real thing. Unless grown in reasonably fertile soil with plenty of organic matter in it, the plants can be rather scrawny and coarse; but, grown well, land cress is invaluable in winter. As in the case of corn salad, plants grown under cover are much more tender.

Cultivation It has to be said that land cress has a slightly cussed streak: perhaps it would be kinder to call it an independent streak. I have often had poor results from sowing it, but on the other hand plants which have run to seed unnoticed in spring have produced a wonderful crop of gleaming little seedlings in the autumn, which I have then transplanted. Land cress is quite tolerant of shade, and grows happily among Brussels sprouts and other winter brassicas – as will corn salad.

Sow seed in July and August for the winter outdoor crop, or in early September for a greenhouse crop. Either sow *in situ*, spacing plants about

9 inches (22.5 cm) apart each way, or sow in seedtrays and transplant. Make sure that the soil is moist for summer sowings, and watch out for flea beetle attacks in the early stages. The flea beetles nibble holes in the very young leaves, but are easily stopped with derris dust.

Lettuces

There are a handful of traditional lettuce varieties which are considered hardy enough to overwinter outdoors, for cutting in spring any time between March and May. These include the winter cos lettuces such as 'Winter Density', butterheads like 'Valdor' and 'Arctic King' and the reddish 'Continuity'. They will be killed off in a severe winter, but it is a gamble worth taking, especially in mild parts of the country. Of course, if any of these lettuces are grown under cover – in cloches, frames, greenhouse or tunnel – their chances of survival are increased enormously, and they will mature earlier and be of far better quality.

In addition to these well known types there are several continental lettuces, often of the non-hearting 'Salad Bowl' (oak leaf) type, which are hardier than people realise. Strangely a lot of them are reddish or bronze-leaved: in fact so many rugged plants have a red streak that I feel there may well be a link between red pigment and hardiness. In this category are 'Red Salad Bowl' and 'Green Salad Bowl', 'Red Lollo' and 'Green Lollo' (very pretty lettuces with curly leaves), 'Red Parella' and 'Green Parella' (very hardy, miniature, Italian lettuces) and 'Marvel of Four Seasons', 'Rougette du Midi' and 'Bruna di Germania' (reddish brown, old, continental varieties). They can all be sown at the end of August and early September, and can be planted outdoors or under cover to get improved, earlier cropping.

With the 'Salad Bowl' and 'Lollo' types and 'Marvel of Four Seasons' a very late sowing can be made under cover in September for a cut-and-come-again seedling crop. Sow either broadcast or in wide drills as suggested for cornsalad. Sometimes the young leaves can be cut once or even twice before winter sets in. They will stop growing in mid-winter, but start into fresh growth early in spring, at a time when colourful salad leaves are a scarce commodity.

Many of the more unusual hardy lettuces are available from Suffolk Herbs and the Henry Doubleday Research Association (see page 21 for addresses).

Reverting to familiar lettuces, I feel we should be a little more daring with 'Little Gem', deservedly one of our most popular lettuces on account of its crispy texture and wonderful sweet flavour. Being a 'semi-cos', it is related to the hardy 'Winter Density' types and, I think, is much hardier than it is presumed to be. Most seed catalogues don't suggest sowing after July, but we keep sowing until at least October. The very latest sowings are either overwintered under cover in seedtrays in readiness for planting out very early in spring, or are planted under cover. In unpleasant, damp winters they may get fungal diseases, it is true, but normally at least half of them survive, and are such a bonus in early spring.

Peas

Peas are another case where a few hardy varieties are traditionally sown outdoors in late autumn, for the first crop the following year. 'Feltham First', 'Beagle' and 'Douce Provence' are among them. In my experience these well-tried varieties can be joined by the mangetout sugar pea types (where the whole immature pod is eaten) and the sugar snap types (where the pod is 'welded' to very sweet, swollen peas inside). I've found them to be as hardy as and much tastier than the standard overwintering peas.

Cultivation I sow peas outdoors in November, sometimes pre-germinating the seed indoors to give them a quick start. I pre-germinate them on a saucer or dish, on moist kitchen paper laid over a base of foam rubber (the latter helps keep them moist). After a day or two the seeds sprout and can then be sown carefully in the ground. I sow them in a patch, spacing the seeds a couple of inches apart each way, rather than in rows. The patch is then surrounded with wire or sheep netting, the closely sown peas giving each other considerable support.

Measures have to be taken to protect these outdoor crops from mice and birds. We set mousetraps among them, covered with a tile or in a drainpipe to keep them dry and make them less accessible to cats. Netting is draped over the top as defence against birds.

If you have space in a greenhouse or polythene tunnel, try sowing a few mange-tout or sugar snap peas under cover. Both are available in dwarf varieties which are a little easier to manage. I've been very successful with sowings made in late November and very early December, which have given me wonderful pickings in late May and early June. Obviously this is impractical if you need all your greenhouse space for early plantings of tomatoes and so on. You will still have to watch out for mice: they even nibble the young pea leaves if they get a chance, they are quite delicious!

Sorrel

If I lived in a city and had only a small garden, I would plant sorrel to give me something green during the winter months. It is easily grown and versatile: a few leaves in a salad add an interesting lemony tang, it can be made into exciting sauces and excellent soup, and it can be cooked like spinach, though it is best mixed with chard or spinach for substance.

In mild winters it stays green; in severe winters it will probably die back at some point, though if it is covered with cloches or a low polythene tunnel its dormant period will either be prevented or very short-lived. It is a tolerant plant, growing quite well in part-shade and in poorish soil, though admittedly doing much better in fertile soil.

You will probably get most value for money by growing one of the broad-leaved French sorrel types. They grow about 1 ft (30 cm) tall, and up to about 3 ft (1 m) when running to seed. (You can still harvest single leaves off the main stem.) But the low-growing 'buckler leaved' sorrel, with its tiny, very strongly flavoured heart-shaped leaves, makes an excellent ground-cover plant.

Cultivation Sorrel can be grown either as an annual or as a perennial; in the latter case the plants should be renewed every 3 or 4 years. Sow from spring to late summer, either *in situ* or in seedboxes and transplanting. If growing as an annual, space plants about 4 inches (10 cm) apart, harvesting the whole plant. Perennial plants can be about 1 ft (30 cm) apart. It is advisable to cut back the seed heads when the plants start to bolt in summer, though you can always leave a couple of plants to seed. Provided the soil is moist, seedlings will root happily, and they can easily be transplanted elsewhere if necessary in spring or autumn.

Texsel Greens

Texsel greens are one of the few new vegetables to appear in recent years, having been developed from an oil seed crop grown in Ethiopia. They belong to the brassica family, and have several good qualities which should recommend them to amateur gardeners.

First, they are very fast-growing and harvested young, so they can be grown in clubroot-infected soil where brassica growing would normally be ruled out. The plants are cut and cleared before there is time for them to become infected.

Second, they are very hardy: in my garden they have survived temperatures as low as 20°F (−6.6°C). Generally speaking, they grow best in the coolish weather of autumn and spring.

Third, they are exceptionally nutritious and have an excellent flavour, either raw or cooked: I'd describe it as part-cabbage and part-spinach, with a faint hint of garlic. If cooking, treat them gently, boiling or steaming for no more than 4 or 5 minutes.

Texsel greens can be eaten at various stages of their growth, from leafy seedlings a couple of inches high to plants 8–12 inches (20–30 cm) tall and not unlike unhearted spring cabbage in appearance.

Cultivation For an autumn/early winter crop sow *in situ* in late summer and early autumn. If you want to use the greens as large seedlings in salads, sow broadcast or in wide drills, as suggested for corn salad. Seedlings can sometimes be cut within 3 weeks of sowing. If you prefer to grow larger plants for 'greens', grow in rows 1 ft (30 cm) apart, thinning to about 1 inch (2.5 cm) apart in the rows; or, if more convenient, in rows 6 inches (15 cm) apart, thinning to 2 inches (5 cm) apart. This is a crop which flea beetles go for, so dust with derris powder if necessary.

I sometimes make an early sowing of Texsel greens in February or March, in a corner of the polythene tunnel or under cloches. This comes in very handy in spring when you start to pine for tasty greens.

Texsel greens seed is available from D.T. Brown (address on page 21).

Oriental Greens

One of my 'discoveries' of recent years has been the treasure trove of oriental vegetables, mainly brassicas, which can be grown in our gardens. They have several advantages over our traditional brassicas. For a start, they are very fast-growing, often ready in a matter of weeks rather than months. They fit in well with the average vegetable garden, as in most cases the best time for sowing and planting is from July to September. (Many have a tendency to bolt from earlier sowings.) They can therefore follow on after the early peas, broad beans, potatoes and so on are lifted.

These greens are high-yielding and flexible and can be harvested at any stage from seedlings to mature crops. In addition the young flowering shoots can be eaten like purple sprouting broccoli when they start to bolt in spring. They are sweet and can be eaten raw in salads.

Last but not least, several are extremely hardy. Even so, I like to have a few plants in my polythene tunnel in winter, sown *in situ* or planted in September. They will grow far more lusciously than the outdoor plants, and go a long way towards bridging the spring vegetable gap, providing fresh greens in mid-winter.

Incidentally, the best way of cooking almost any oriental brassica is stir-frying. This *can* be done in a large frying-pan or heavy saucepan, but is much easier in a wok. To stir-fry, cut the greens into even-sized pieces (stemmy pieces can be 1 inch (2.5 cm) or so long and should be cooked a little longer than leafy parts). Heat the wok and put in a couple of tablespoons of cooking oil. When it has warmed up, lightly fry a little garlic and ginger in it, if you like their flavour. Then add the vegetables, stirring them gently as they cook. Sometimes they will be tender enough after a couple of minutes' cooking. If they look on the dry side, add a little water, turn the heat down low, cover the wok with a lid and allow them more or less to steam for a couple of minutes more. This method of cooking is excellent for preserving the colour, flavour and nutrients of vegetables.

Mizuna Greens

Also known as Japanese greens, Japanese mustard or kyona, this is a very pretty plant with glossy, dark green, serrated leaves, growing 9–12 inches (22.5–30 cm) high. Its hardiness is on a par with that of spring cabbage, though it is more apt to be killed by the cold mushiness of melting snow than straight low temperatures. In the winter of 1988/89 a border of mizuna plants in my small decorative vegetable garden was a picture from November to early summer. In summer mizuna tolerates light shade, and I often plant it beneath sweetcorn: not only is this pretty but the mizuna plants remain productive long after the sweetcorn has been harvested.

Cultivation Mizuna can be sown earlier than most oriental greens, but for winter use sow any time from July to September. For use raw in salads, sow in narrow or wide drills as for corn salad (page 13), cutting the young fern-like leaves when 2–4 inches (5–10 cm) high. Mizuna is naturally vigorous and in most conditions the plants can be cut several times over a long period, though the leaves get rather coarse in very hot weather.

Alternatively, aim for larger plants, sowing *in situ*, or in seedboxes and planting out about 9 inches (22.5 cm) apart. These larger leaves are better cooked: they have a pleasant, slightly mustard flavour, and are excellent mixed with other oriental greens.

Green-in-the-Snow Mustard

Green-in-the-snow mustard was one of the first oriental brassicas to be introduced to the West and, as the name implies, it is exceptionally hardy. It really *is* green in the snow, though funnily enough the literal translation of the Chinese name is 'red in the snow'! The rather shaggy leaves are pleasantly spicy when young and can be eaten raw; the older leaves become too peppery to eat raw, though are excellent cooked.

Cultivation Sow in August for a winter crop, either *in situ* or in boxes. Plants can either be spaced 4–5 inches (10–12.5 cm) apart and harvested very young, or spaced about 8 inches (20 cm) apart and allowed to grow larger. As with all these vegetables, the leaves will be more tender if they are given cloche or low tunnel protection in winter. Once warm weather comes in spring, they run to seed rapidly and the leaves grow too hot-flavoured for use.

Komatsuna (Spinach Mustard)

This is a large group of brassicas, closely related to turnips. Some have huge, glossy leaves, some duller leaves, but they are wonderfully vigorous, extremely hardy and very pleasantly flavoured. They can be sown in wide drills and cut as seedlings about 4 inches (10 cm) high, or allowed to develop into large plants. The flowering shoots in spring are delicious. Available varieties include 'Tendergreen' and 'All Top' or 'Big Top'. Every

winter I grow a few plants outdoors and some in the polythene tunnel, and I also make a very early sowing for a cut-and-come-again seedling crop in spring under cover or outdoors as soon as the soil is workable.
Cultivation Sow in August or September, in the same way as mizuna. For large plants space the seedlings 12–14 inches (30–35 cm) apart.

Spring Seedlings of Oriental Brassicas

One of the best ways of getting exceptionally fresh green leaves early in spring for salads or cooking is to sow oriental brassicas under low polythene tunnels or cloches as early in the year as the ground is workable, for cutting as leafy seedlings a couple of inches high. This works a treat with any varieties of pak choi (the seedlings have wonderfully crunchy stems), with the non-heading Chinese cabbages like serrated and round santo, with mizuna and komatsuna, and with Chinese cabbage, though in the last case you need to cook the leaves: they are on the tough side to eat raw!

Sowing broadcast or in wide drills to get these seedling crops requires more seed than is normally supplied in a single packet. Suffolk Herbs can supply larger packets. For mature plants for winter sow in August or September and thin or transplant to 12–14 inches (30–35 cm) apart.

◆ MAIL ORDER SEED SUPPLIERS ◆

Boyce, J. W.
237 Carter Street,
Fordham,
Cambridgeshire CB7 5JU.
General list.

Suffolk Herbs,
Sawyers Farm, Little Cornard,
Sudbury, Suffolk CO10 0NY.
Wide range of unusual salad, herb, vegetable and flower seed.

Henry Doubleday Research Assoc.,
National Centre for Organic
Gardening, Ryton-on-Dunsmore,
Coventry CV8 3LG.
Vegetable, herb and salad seed.

Chiltern Seeds,
Bortree Stile,
Ulverston, Cumbria LA12 7PB.
Oriental vegetables and unusual seed.

Brown, D. T. & Co.
Poulton-le-Fylde,
Blackpool FY6 7HY.
General list and Texsel greens.

Unwins Seeds,
Histon, Cambridge CB4 4LE.
General list and some orientals.

Suttons Seeds,
Hele Road, Torquay, Devon TQ2 7QJ.
General list and some orientals.

Thompson & Morgan,
London Road, Ipswich IP2 0BA.
General list and some orientals.

Fothergill Seeds,
Gazeley Road,
Kentford, Newmarket,
Suffolk CB8 7QB.
General list and some orientals.

◆ FRAMES ◆

by Geoff Hamilton

The first recorded cold-frame was used by the Emperor Tiberius in the first century. It seems that the good life did nothing for the poor fellow's digestion, so he needed to consume quantities of cucumber to set it right. He grew his cucumbers on hot-beds made with horse manure and the plants were covered with frames glazed with mica or talc.

We may look askance at the Romans' medical theories, but we have to admit that they were no mean gardeners. That technique of using frames heated by hot-beds lasted for many centuries and was later perfected by the Victorians.

◆ USES ◆

Because of our climate, a cold-frame is much more use to us than ever it would have been to the Romans. If you raise plants in a greenhouse, it's more or less essential in order gradually to acclimatise plants grown in heated conditions to the lower temperatures outside. It can also be used to raise early vegetables and flowers in spring and exotic fruit and vegetables in the summer. Even in winter it will provide protection for a wide range of crops to enable harvesting to take place much earlier the next year. A new frame may cost a few bob, but it'll very quickly repay its cost, increase the scope of your gardening and give you hours of pleasure too.

◆ CHOOSING A FRAME ◆

Of course, modern cold-frames have progressed well beyond the stage of mica and talc. They now consist of either a wooden base topped by a glass or plastic lid, or an aluminium frame glazed throughout.

A wooden frame will give more protection from frost and cold weather during the winter. So, if it's to be used to overwinter seedlings or cuttings, for example, wood is to be preferred. However, because of the wooden sides, there's naturally less available light than you'd get from an all-glass frame. Often that doesn't matter. If you want to use it, say, purely for propagating, it'll need to be shaded most of the time anyway. But if you want to grow seedlings or young plants for any length of time in the spring and summer, an all-glass job is the best bet.

It's also possible to buy cold-frames that are very sophisticated indeed.

There are fairly tall structures available which can even rival a greenhouse – except, of course, that, though the plants stay warm, the gardener must remain out in the cold! My own (admittedly limited) experience of them is that they tend to overheat in summer and are quite difficult to ventilate.

The addition of heat is quite an advantage if you haven't got a greenhouse, but again, because the space is small, there's less margin for error, so you have to be quite careful. However, I've found that *bottom* heat can be very useful indeed, especially if you're a keen propagator. It really does make all the difference to the successful rooting of cuttings, especially if it can be combined with automatic misting. All these systems are available and can easily be adapted to fit any make of frame.

When buying a cold-frame, make sure that you can ventilate it adequately. As I've already suggested, the small volume of air inside leaves little room for error and temperatures can fluctuate wildly, especially in the early spring. I experimented a little last spring, with a maximum/minimum thermometer in an empty frame. Thank goodness it was empty, because temperatures on a sunny day followed by a freezing night ranged from 110°F (43°C) to 19°F (−7°C). Plants can often get used to slightly too high a temperature or even get hardened to survive a few degrees below normal, but that kind of fluctuation spells instant death.

◆ SITING ◆

For the same reason, you should avoid the sunniest spot when siting your frame, unless you can give it constant attention. If you have to go out to work in the morning, you'll need to be quite a weather prophet to assess how much to ventilate. But, if the frame's in a light spot but out of direct sunlight, temperatures will be inclined to fluctuate less. However, try to avoid putting it underneath trees. Constant dripping from above will soon make the glass green and murky, and when you remove the top the plants inside will be damaged too.

If you're going to use the frame just for propagating, a shady spot is to be preferred. In winter beneath a west-facing wall is ideal, while in summer the north side is preferable. Of course, one of the advantages of a cold frame is that it's easy to move about.

◆ HOME-MADE FRAMES ◆

Making your own cold-frame is well within the scope of the not-terribly-handy handyman or handywoman. Indeed, I've rooted literally hundreds of cuttings of shrubs and herbaceous plants in a 'frame' which cost me 7p and took about five minutes to make. I must admit that it has to be firmly placed in the lower end of the range, but it works.

It consists of an old apple box begged from Bob, my friendly green-grocer. (He's the man who once complained, 'Why do I keep giving you bits and pieces from my shop so that you can tell other people how *not* to have to buy their fruit and vegetables?') I bought a scrap of rigid plastic from the DIY shop for the top and that was held on with a length of nylon twine and a strong elastic band. I made it seven years ago and it's still in use, so I reckon I've recouped my investment by now. That's just 1p a year!

To cover all eventualities I also knocked up a couple of different designs. These are 'proper' cold-frames and have been used to grow a wide variety of vegetables, to raise seedlings and to strike cuttings. I've made the construction very simple indeed because, believe me, I'm no Chippendale. You need a saw, hammer, screwdriver and a sharp knife.

The first design is for a wooden-sided frame made with floorboards. If you buy new timber from the builder's merchant, it'll set you back about £20, but you can easily halve that cost with second-hand timber from the demolition contractor's yard. If you haven't paid him a visit, I strongly urge you to do so, because all such places are real Aladdin's caves of good materials for gardeners at a fraction of the cost of new.

The top panel can be made from rigid PVC which is readily available at the DIY store. It has two disadvantages: it's quite expensive and it's not easy to work with. It does tend to shatter easily, so you'll need a special tool to cut it (very cheap at the DIY shop) and you'll have to drill holes and screw it to the wooden frame. When you do, make sure that you have a washer under each screw, because just tightening it up is enough to crack it. It has the great advantage that it's crystal-clear so you can see inside at a glance, and it looks good in the garden too.

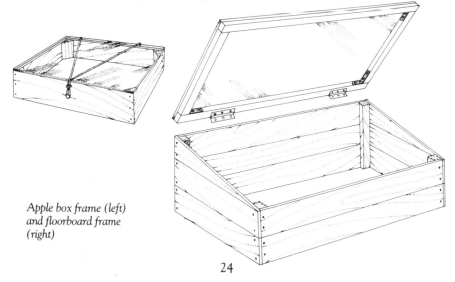

Apple box frame (left) and floorboard frame (right)

24

The alternative is corrugated plastic sold as Correx. This is super material because you can cut it with a knife and simply tack it on to the wooden frame. It's also considerably cheaper, but it has the disadvantage of being opaque, so you can't see your plants without opening it and it does tend to stand out a bit in a small garden. You pays your money and you takes your choice.

The wooden frame used to hold the plastic for the lid is made from roofing lathes. These you'll get from the builder's merchant very cheaply, and they're held together at the corners by metal angle brackets. And that's the system that forms the basis for building the second design.

This is the one to make if you want to grow plants that need all the light possible, at least early in their growing cycle. Things like tomatoes, melons, lettuce and so on do better in this type of frame because of the increased light.

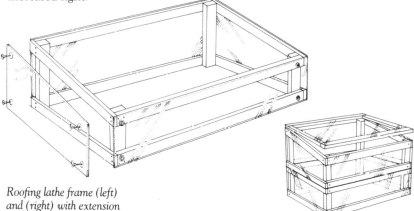

Roofing lathe frame (left)
and (right) with extension

The snag, of course, with a conventional cold-frame is its restricted height. It's fine for low growers like lettuce, melons, cucumbers or bush tomatoes, but when it comes to upright tomatoes, peppers or aubergines, it's severely limiting. So I also made an extension that fits underneath the frame. When the plants get tall enough to need more room, you can just slip the extension underneath. Don't make the mistake of putting it on right from the start since this will tend to draw the young plants upwards. The extension has, of course, to be made from plastic because wood would make it much too murky inside.

♦ HEATING ♦

There's no doubt that you can greatly increase the versatility of your frame if you add a little heat. You can buy small, tubular, electric heaters to warm the air space, but the best bet in my view is to supply the heat underneath the plants with a soil-warming cable.

You can buy this in various lengths and simply lay it into a bed of sand, arranging it in serpentine fashion to cover the bottom of the frame. If you like, you can also run it round the wall of the frame to provide a little air warming too. Ideally, link it to a rod thermostat in the side of the frame. This system is marvellous for taking cuttings and for forcing on the earliest vegetable crops.

◆ MAKING THE BEST OF THE COLD-FRAME ◆

The Vegetable Frame

It's possible to keep the frame full of vegetables alone for most of the year. The advantages with growing vegetables in this way are that you'll be harvesting them a few weeks earlier than the open-ground stuff and also that the quality will be much higher. This is especially true of plants grown during winter and early spring.

Start the year in early February, sowing a quick-maturing lettuce like 'Tom Thumb'. The plants can be thinned out to 6 inches (15 cm) apart as soon as the seedlings are large enough to handle; and the thinnings too can be transplanted.

At the same time you could sow a row or two of early carrots like 'Amsterdam Forcing' or 'Rondo'. These won't need thinning if they're sown thinly enough, but should be pulled selectively to allow space for those remaining to increase in size.

Use the same technique with turnip 'Milan Purple Top', which will quickly produce some small, succulent turnips in the latter part of April. Spring onions will fill a little space and need not be thinned either.

If you have room, cabbage 'Hispi' and cauliflower 'Alpha Polaris' can be sown too and transplanted or thinned to about 9 inches (22.5 cm) apart.

I would also try to find space for a row of spinach. It produces quickly and is most welcome early in the season. Broad beans can be brought forward as well, but they do need at least 18 inches (45 cm) in height.

Of course, any spare space can be regularly filled with a patch of radish. Sown thinly, they won't need thinning either.

In late April or early May, those first crops will be out of the way and you can re-plant with more exotic stuff. Courgettes, bush tomatoes, melons, cucumbers, peppers and aubergines can all be raised in the greenhouse or on the windowsill and will crop well in the cold-frame. Plant them all about 18 inches (45 cm) apart. They'll take a little while to fill their allotted space, so you could still grow a quick crop of carrots or lettuce while they're thinking about it. Make sure that you use an early-maturing variety again, though.

That lot should be gone by August and then you can sow a winter lettuce like 'Novita' or 'Kellys'. If the weather's hot, try to shade the frame because the seed won't germinate if the soil temperature is higher than 68°F (20°C). They'll overwinter and be the first lettuce you cut in the new year.

At that time you can also start off cauliflower 'All the Year Round' for a very early cutting in spring.

I certainly wouldn't miss out on strawberries, which can be brought on by several weeks in the frame, enabling you to enjoy them when they're at their most expensive in the shops. If you aren't anticipating a lot of room in spring, I would plant up the strawberries in 6 inch (15 cm) pots. Do that in August if you can and then put them outside in a place where they won't get waterlogged. They need a cold spell to initiate fruit, so don't bring them into the frame until February. When they look as though they've started growing again, give them a feed of tomato fertiliser and, if you take your own early strawberries to Wimbledon, you'll pay for the frame at a stroke!

Hardening off

Tender plants grown in a greenhouse for planting outside in late May or early June must first be acclimatised or 'hardened off'. To put them straight outside, even after all danger of frost has gone, can often give a severe check to their growth. And, once any plant stops growing, it's quite a job to get it going again.

Generally you would start putting plants into the cold-frame in late April. Start with the frame completely closed for a few days. Keep a watchful eye on the weather forecast, and if a severe frost is threatened, cover the frame with sacking or a piece of old carpet at night.

After a few days, the frame can be opened a little during the day and closed again at night. This daily opening should be increased over the next weeks until the frame is opened completely during the day. At night it should be kept closed until about the middle of May and then gradually and progressively opened a little more each night. The plants can be finally removed in the last week of May in the south and the first or second week in June in the north.

It's obvious that this advice is just a rough guide. You'll still need to keep an eagle eye open for freak cold spells and, if you live in an exposed spot, you may have to start hardening off later. The most convenient way to prop the lid open is with a stepped block of wood, easily made from a piece of scrap.

Propagating

Many seeds can be started in the cold-frame without heat. All the hardy annuals, including subjects like marigolds, godetia, clarkia, annual lupin and so on, can be started in March when it's still much too wet and cold to sow them outside. I use polystyrene Propapacks and sow a tiny pinch of seed to each cell. I don't bother thinning out when they come through but just plant out each block as if it were a single plant. They come much earlier and make better plants than those sown direct. And there aren't any spaces in the borders either.

Sweet peas can be sown in special tubes or in rolls of newspaper held together with a paper clip. Sow them either in November or in February/March. I have never noticed much difference in the quality of the plants either way, so I generally leave mine until spring.

Other seeds like alpines and certain trees can be sown in pots in the frame, but bear in mind that some need to be frozen, so leave the lid propped open all the time. The advantage with the frame is that it excludes the worst of the wet and enables you to keep mice and birds away from your seeds and plants by stretching a piece of wire or plastic netting over the top. It's also easier to shade seedlings in summer, if they are in a frame.

In summer the frame should be packed with all manner of cuttings. Herbaceous plants are, in the main, pretty easy to root at this time of year and many will do so without any special care. Just take a shoot about 2 inches (5 cm) long, remove the bottom leaves so that just two or at the most three remain on the top, and insert it into a pot of compost made from equal parts of sphagnum peat and vermiculite. Then stand it in the closed frame and shade it from hot sun with a piece of greenhouse shading netting.

Shrubs and conifers take a little more trouble. Here it's best to take the cuttings in June or July, using the soft, young growth that has been made that year. Prepare the cuttings in the same way as herbaceous ones, but dip the whole thing first into a solution of fungicide. I use liquid copper or Benlate, but almost any fungicide will do. The reason for it is that the cuttings take longer to root so are more prone to attack from mildew.

Then dip the end into *fresh* hormone rooting powder (it does go off after about a year) and dibble the cuttings into a pot of the same compost suggested for herbaceous plants.

These methods will succeed with a wide range of plants, but there's no doubt that you will be more successful if you add a little heat.

◆ SLUG CONTROL ◆

by Bill Symondson

Britain has few serious pests compared with the tropics, where all vegetation in a whole region can be wiped out by insects such as locusts. However, we do have one non-insect pest that can, under certain circumstances, destroy most of our crops. No gardener needs two guesses as to what this is – it has to be the slug.

When allotment holders were asked recently to name the crops that most frequently suffered from pest attacks, brassicas and potatoes headed the list. In both cases slugs were seen as the main pest responsible, and overall they were blamed for causing the most damage to vegetables. In response to this, slug pellets lead the field as the most used pesticides.

You are probably now thinking that once again a carefully conducted survey has uncovered what we all knew anyway. But perhaps we have more to complain about than you might have realised. Britain is the slug capital of the world. Nowhere else has such ideal conditions for a broad range of slug species, for our cool, damp summers and warmish, wet winters allow slugs to be active, breeding and feeding for so much of the year. Added to this, we have recently suffered a succession of milder winters and cooler, wetter summers. Normally, icy conditions kill off a percentage of slugs and prevent the remainder from breeding and eating our crops for a while. Similarly, hot, dry weather kills slugs, which have to burrow deep into the ground to find the moist conditions that they need to survive. Meanwhile they give us a break – until we get out the hosepipe to water the beans, of course, and bring them all back to the surface!

◆ SLUG IDENTIFICATION ◆

To control any pest it is essential to know something about the beast. In this instance identification of the various types of slug is desirable, because not all of them cause problems in the garden. As explained later, over-use of slug poisons can be counter-productive in that you risk killing off the predators that are helping to control your slug population. Such poisons should therefore be used, if used at all, only when and where a serious problem is seen to be developing, involving a slug species that is known to attack the crop you are growing. Once you have identified the species, and can learn a little about its habits, you might well find that there are non-chemical options that are effective controls.

There are around thirty species of slug in Britain (plus some exotics in glasshouses). Only a minority pose any serious problem, and four of the worst and most numerous of these that cause damage in gardens are described below. For more detailed identification of slugs, you might like to refer to one of the books listed at the end of this chapter.

The Grey Field Slug (*Deroceras reticulatum*)

The grey field slug is small – up to 1½ inches (4 cm) – and usually grey/fawn in colour with darker flecks. It has a short, truncated keel or ridge on the back at the tail end. The underside, or sole, is whitish, with a darker zone along the centre. The mucus is colourless or white.

The grey field slug is a surface-feeding specialist, typically found infesting lettuces and cabbages. In fact it eats almost all our crops, from carrots and beans to spinach and tobacco, from celery and tomatoes to orchids and cacti. It is a major pest of cereal crops, and will even eat potato haulms.

The Garden Slug (*Arion hortensis*)

The garden slug is a small, blackish slug up to 1¼ inches (3 cm), with a paler side stripe. It has no keel and is distinguishable from similar species by its rounded cross section (see Fig. 1). The sole is yellow or orange; the mucus the same colour.

A burrower *and* surface-feeder, the garden slug attacks both leaf and

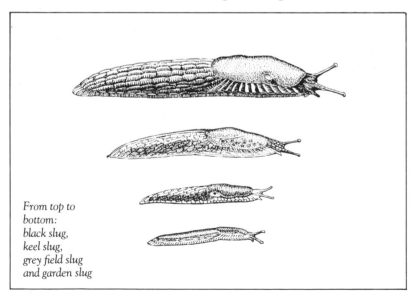

From top to bottom: black slug, keel slug, grey field slug and garden slug

root crops. Typically it attacks at ground level, severing the stems of young beans or marrow plants, for example, but it will also climb up and attack the heads of cauliflowers and many other plants, or burrow down to eat the roots of, say, turnips or beetroot. It is a major pest of potatoes, attacking both tubers and foliage, and has been known to penetrate the soil to as much as a yard's depth, so nothing is safe from this slug.

The Keel Slug *(Milax budapestensis)*

The keel slug is a larger species, up to 2½ inches (6 cm). Usually dark grey/brown in colour, it has a keel, with a yellow or orange stripe along the ridge. The sole is pale, the mucus colourless. Typically it curves into a sickle shape when contracted.

A burrowing specialist, notorious for its destruction of potatoes, it will in fact attack most root crops and is difficult to control as it spends most of its time underground.

The Black Slug *(Arion ater)*

The black slug can be very big: a length of up to 7.87 inches (20 cm) has been recorded. Its colour is very variable – white, red or brown are all common, although black is most usual, often with an orange fringe. There is no keel, and the skin is coarse and granular. The sole is pale, sometimes orange, and the mucus white. The black slug may rock from side to side when disturbed!

Familiar to all gardeners because of its spectacular size, the black slug is rarely as destructive as the three smaller species described above but can cause damage in spring to seedlings of many kinds. Later, when its preferred diet of rotting vegetation, fungi, manure and even dead animals is more readily available, it causes little damage in the garden – other than promoting heart failure if you step on one when feeding the cat at night!

◆ SLUG CONTROL – CHEMICAL ◆

Garden centres make a fortune selling slug pellets – more, probably, than from all the other pesticides put together. Only a fraction of the quantity sold is ever eaten by a slug, and a much smaller proportion will actually cause the death of one. Given also the fact that every year there are reports of pets and wildlife dying or being made seriously ill after eating slug pellets, it seems obvious that these poisons are not being used efficiently, from the point of view either of controlling slugs or of environmental safety.

There are two different active ingredients used in slug pellets – metaldehyde and methiocarb. Both are readily available, although gardeners generally use metaldehyde, while farmers prefer methiocarb.

Metaldehyde Pellets and Spray

Originally metaldehyde was used as a solid fuel (meta-tablets). Its slug-killing properties were accidentally discovered by farmers in southern France, who noticed dead and dying slugs and snails on picnic sites where meta-tablets had been left on the ground.

A metaldehyde slug pellet contains only about 4 per cent of this chemical; the rest is in fact bait, containing a cereal base with various added attractants, such as yeast. Pure metaldehyde actually repels slugs, as will concentrations of pellets, which explains why it is important to spread these thinly. The poison can affect slugs either by contact, with absorption through the skin, or through the gut when eaten. The main effect is that of an irritant, causing the slug to produce masses of mucus, leading to dehydration and sometimes death. Loss of mucus also means that the slug can no longer move around, so that dead and dying slugs are found close to the baiting site.

Unfortunately, this dehydration process can take a day or more to kill the slug. If, during this interval, there is rain, or even a heavy dew, slugs can re-hydrate and make a full recovery. Temperature is also very important. At 44°F (7°C) or below, treatment is likely to fail, particularly in damp conditions. Above 68°F (20°C) a very high percentage of slugs will be killed. There is clearly a 'Catch-22' situation here, for in hot dry weather, when the kill rate is highest, slug activity is lowest, whereas in damp conditions, when slug activity is highest, kill rates are lowest, because there is a high recovery rate!

There is an answer. The best control can be achieved during warm weather. Put down the pellets on a humid evening, when dry weather is expected the next day. Slug activity will then be very high during that night, with a good uptake of bait. By morning the slugs will be paralysed by the poison and unable to move into shelter. The dry day, particularly if it is sunny, will finish them off. If, however, the weather will not co-operate, and cooler or wetter conditions prevail, you will certainly kill fewer slugs, but you will still prevent much of the damage to your crops. This is because slugs that have been partially poisoned are inhibited from feeding for up to a week. Alternatively, you might decide to use methiocarb pellets.

Metaldehyde is broken down by sunlight, so where possible the pellets should be put in shady places, particularly under the leaves of the affected plants – which is where the slugs will be anyway. This chemical can also be applied in spray form, in which case it will act purely as a contact killer, so here too it is important to use it only when slugs are active. About 70 per cent of the slugs that are going to be killed will be poisoned in the first twenty-four hours of treatment. However, even heavy applications are unlikely to reduce your garden slug population, temporarily, by more than

10 per cent. Recently the 'shower resistant' properties of metaldehyde pellets have been improved, increasing the effective life of the pellets in the garden and therefore increasing kill rates.

Methiocarb Pellets and Spray

Methiocarb is one of a group of chemicals called carbamates, which includes herbicides, fungicides and, especially, insecticides. Again, pellets contain around 4 per cent active ingredient, plus cereals and other attractants. They tend to be more expensive and are certainly more poisonous than metaldehyde pellets. Methiocarb is less important as a contact killer, acting more as a stomach poison when eaten.

The advantage of methiocarb is that it is more effective at lower temperatures, and in fact recovery by slugs treated with it is lower in wetter weather – the opposite of the case with metaldehyde. Slugs that have been poisoned can, however, move around for a while, but then swell up with fluid and become immobile, dying shortly afterwards. In dry conditions this swelling can be reduced, and some slugs may recover, although generally recovery rates are lower than with metaldehyde. Methiocarb breaks down more slowly than metaldehyde, which can be both an advantage and a disadvantage (see below).

Pros and Cons of the Two Chemicals

If you must use a chemical slug killer, choose metaldehyde pellets whenever possible. To begin with, methiocarb is also an insecticide, which means that it will kill many of the predatory beetles which are themselves helping to control your garden slugs. As these beetles take longer to recover their numbers than do the slugs, you might well be making matters worse in the long run. Methiocarb is about ten times as poisonous to mammals as metaldehyde, so it is a dangerous chemical to have around yourselves or your food. In practice, however, it is often the less poisonous metaldehyde that is responsible for the death of pets and wildlife. Dogs can become addicted to the pellets and some will actively seek them out with fatal consequences. Methiocarb, because it is so poisonous, will frequently make an animal ill before it has had time to take in a fatal dose. Worms can be killed by it and, at least in spray form, it may affect the growth of some plants.

From a garden wildlife point of view, therefore, slug pellets of either type are bad news. Birds and hedgehogs may be killed not only by eating the pellets, but also by eating the poisoned slugs. The formulation of slug pellets is very like that for dog food, with added poison, so it is little wonder that they are eaten by creatures other than those at which they are aimed. Indeed, the Ministry of Agriculture once advised the use of slug pellets for the control of small mammals on farms. The majority of poisonings of pets seen by vets are as a consequence of slug pellet use.

So the message is: use methiocarb only in a real emergency where slugs are devastating a crop under prolonged, cold, wet conditions and when no alternative system seems to work. Otherwise choose metaldehyde – or non-chemical methods.

Using Pellets Efficiently and Safely

It is an important principle of pest control that the minimum dose that will do the job should be used. Pesticide that does not reach its target will undermine the overall effectiveness of your control measures, in this case by harming your garden 'friends', the predators and parasites of slugs and other pests.

As a rule of thumb, a maximum of eighty mini pellets per square yard should be used – that is, there should be about 4 inches (10 cm) between each one. Spread them any more densely and most will not be taken up, while the repellant effect may actually reduce the kill, particularly where small heaps are used. Choose the evening before a warm, humid night if possible. Confine the use of pellets to limited areas. The edges of walls, paths and lawns are the sorts of places in which slugs like to hide away during the day, where they can find damp, dark, cool refuges. When using pellets in a crop, do not throw them around wildly or you run the risk of some lodging in plants and contaminating your food. If at all practicable, protect birds and hedgehogs from the pellets by using netting. Pea guards are particularly suitable for 'edge situations', and are easy to manage. It is a very good idea to remove and kill any slugs found around the pellets the next day because many will be paralysed but not dead and could recover if rain follows treatment. You can skim off the pellets and slugs for disposal, which will allow you to move the guards and treat another section, for if conditions were right you will have killed most of the slugs you were going to kill in that area on the first night. Such speedy treatment, and removal of chemicals, will minimise the risks to non-target creatures.

There are no stated safety periods in this country between treatment and eating associated crops. However, such restrictions apply elsewhere in Europe and it would be wise to err on the side of caution and wait at least a week – even longer if you have used methiocarb spray.

Metaldehyde Tapes and Pads

Metaldehyde tapes and pads have been developed in recent years to try to retain the benefits of using this chemical while eliminating some of the disadvantages.

The tapes come in the form of coils, a little like recording tape but made of paper. In fact they consist of a sandwich of paper with metaldehyde as the filling! In order to get a dose of the filling, slugs have to eat the paper, which is impregnated with various secret ingredients to make it tasty (to slugs!). The paper is water-repellent so that it can go on working over a long period. The idea is that by the time the paper has rotted, the metaldehyde too will have broken down chemically into harmless constituents and thus will not pollute the soil. Unlike pellets, the tapes do not contain a large amount of cereal and are thus not so attractive to birds and other wildlife. Predatory insects too seem to leave them alone, although all these creatures could, of course, be poisoned 'second hand' by eating dead or dying slugs.

The tapes must be laid out in strips alongside rows of crops, or in circles around cherished plants, such as hostas. In order to stop them blowing about, weight them with stones every 5 inches (12 cm) or so.

The main disadvantage seems to be that birds, scratching about on the soil, will soon mess up your nicely ordered tapes, so you have to go around regularly pegging them out again. Worms also cause trouble from below, pulling the tapes down into their burrows by the yard and shredding them! This cannot be doing the worms any good and, of course, causes some of the chemical to contaminate the soil. These objections aside, the tapes are certainly an improvement on pellets in ecological terms and thus worth the additional cost.

The pads work in much the same way, but underground. These small squares of metaldehyde 'sandwich' should be buried along with your seed potatoes to give long lasting protection against keel slugs and garden slugs. They can also be used in walls, rockeries and similarly difficult locations, particularly against snails.

Aluminium Sulphate and Copper Sulphate

Copper sulphate has long been used with great success in tropical countries to clear disease-carrying snails from ditches and lakes, although it can damage water plants and fish. If you use it for slugs, keep it well away from ponds. For slugs, this chemical is used in spray form. It has been found to be effective against the small grey field slug when sprayed on to the soil, but less so against other species. It is a contact poison, and should thus be used only when slugs are active – as they crawl about, they pick up a dose. It is quickly washed down by rain, so repeated treatments are often necessary. However, because a build-up of copper in the soil can seriously affect worm numbers, repeated use is not recommended.

Aluminium sulphate has until recently been considered almost 'organic', and as such has been widely used. It too is effective only against very small slugs, particularly grey field slugs, which are more susceptible than other species to contact poisons. Again, treatment should be confined to times when slugs are most active, and repeated use is often necessary. Aluminium sulphate has received a bad press since large quantities of this chemical were accidentally released into the water supply in Cornwall, causing health problems for many people. There is no evidence that the small amounts possibly absorbed by plants in treated areas of your garden would ever produce similar effects. However, there is a question mark over the connection between aluminium and Alzheimer's disease, or senile dementia. The risks can be minimised by keeping the spray off the foliage. With seedlings this is vitally important as they can be killed by direct spraying.

There are various mixtures of aluminium and copper sulphates on the market, with or without various additional salts and herbal extracts. There is little evidence that they work better than either chemical on its own.

◆ SLUG CONTROL – NON-CHEMICAL ◆

I have deliberately not called this non-chemical slug control 'organic' because all the techniques are applicable to both organic and conventional systems. Indeed, the use of chemicals would rarely be adequate protection alone.

Barriers

A number of different materials can be used to surround plants with the intention of deterring slugs. Most, like sand, ashes, broken eggshells and soot, are physically difficult for slugs to get across, either through being scratchy and sharp or by drying up the mucous glands that are necessary for their movement. There may sometimes be a chemically repellent effect too, as, for instance, in the case of ashes.

Unfortunately, these substances all suffer from the ravages of wind and rain, which respectively blow the stuff about or splash it with mud. In addition weeds may grow up and form bridges for slugs on the soil's surface, while the burrowers have no trouble going underneath in any case! However, with plenty of maintenance such barriers can work against surface-feeding species, particularly if other, more easily accessible food is available near by.

A surface mulch of mixed stable manure and wood chips has been found by some gardeners to be an effective slug deterrent, while others have discovered that this, and composted bark, attract slugs. It may depend again on what choice is offered to the slugs, and on weather conditions. Tannins in the bark might have a repellent effect, while drying of the surface might slow them down a little. More experimental work is needed on this.

Plastic barriers can be used in various ways to create walls against slug attack, although admittedly they can be unsightly. In the simplest form, a clear plastic bottle with top and bottom cut off to form a cylinder can be used to protect small plants, such as young brassicas. Otherwise, semi-rigid, thick, clear plastic can be inserted, on edge, into the soil to form a wall around a whole group of plants. The above-ground wall should be at least 8 inches (20 cm) high, while the below-ground section should be at least 4 inches (10 cm) deep. The walls can, if necessary, be supported by pieces of cane or pipe. Such barriers will not be 100 per cent slug-proof, but at least they will reduce the 'slug pressure'. Of course, you must be sure that you are not trapping slugs that may already be in the plot you want to protect.

Beer or Milk Traps

Smooth glass or plastic containers, sunk into the soil and filled with beer or milk, certainly trap slugs. However there are problems. Never, for instance, sink the containers with their rims flush with the soil level. If you do, you will drown ground beetles that are important pest (including slug) controllers. The rims should be ½–¾ inch (1–2 cm) above the soil's surface (*right*): slugs can crawl up and over quite easily. For this method to be an effective control, you need an awful lot of beer traps – at the very least one every yard in each direction – and an awful lot of beer or milk. The liquid must be replenished every few days, which can be quite a task. However, on a small scale, to protect a group of choice plants, the technique can work.

Night Time by Torch Light

This method of slug extermination is strictly for the non-squeamish. Fix a hat pin, or similar needle-like item, to a stick, binding it tightly with string. Then simply go round the garden spearing your slugs like the man collecting litter in the park. The slugs can be transferred to a container of salt or boiling water to finish them off. It sounds rather horrible, but at least, if you are worried, you can be sure that in this way they have a quicker death than would be the case with any of the poisons. One can become quite hard-hearted when an expensive and long-sought hosta is turned to lace the night after planting.

This technique can be surprisingly successful. Whereas a beer trap might catch a dozen or so slugs in a week, you can easily kill a couple of hundred an hour by searching. The greatest numbers are usually to be found on the lawn and pathways rather than on the soil itself. If you don't mind remarks about your waning sanity, you could even mow the lawn at night – you would kill slugs by the thousand! There might be lighting and safety problems, however, so take care – and warn the neighbours.

Cultivation, Drainage, Soil Conditioning

Soil rotovation, in early spring and between crops, is one of the best of all slug controls. Three passes with a rotovator across an area of soil should reduce slug numbers to about a quarter of their previous level. This can, therefore, be more effective than any of the chemical treatments. Choose a time when the weather is warming up, to ensure that the slugs are at or near the soil's surface. Obviously the soil must not be too wet and claggy, or you will end up with a sticky mess. Rotovation both physically kills slugs and also exposes them and their eggs to predators and the weather. Digging by hand will have the same result to a lesser extent, and may be necessary where rotovating is inappropriate – on raised beds, for instance.

Slugs like heavy, wet soils, particularly for laying their eggs, to ensure that they do not dry out. They also like a rough surface with plenty of soil spaces to hide in. If the ground is covered with weeds as well, they think they are in paradise! So obviously it pays to avoid such conditions. Wet ground should be drained where possible, or avoided for the growing of slug-sensitive plants. Raised beds can be useful in combating the problems of heavy ground as they provide that little bit of extra height which improves drainage. In some circumstances coarse grit can help to improve a soil, as can well-rotted manure or compost (if it is not well rotted, slugs will home in from all directions). Try to obtain a good tilth as early as possible in the season. This destroys the soil crack refuges and creates a surface that will dry out and be unattractive to slugs. Get rid of weeds such as dandelions that provide not only food but also refuges for slugs among your plants. A fine, firm seedbed is required ideally. Minimal digging systems are almost always plagued by slugs, partly because of the lack of cultivation and partly because of associated crop residues.

Controlled Refuges

If you have followed the advice given so far, you will have clear, smooth, weed-free beds with very little cover, particularly in spring. To encourage ground-living insect predators within the beds, you will need to provide artificial refuges. Old wooden boards are best and neatest (*below*), but small pieces of carpet, slates and so on will also do. The predators hide under these during the day, emerging at night to perform their duty.

I call these hiding places 'controlled refuges' because they have another important function. If you look underneath once a week, you will find slugs hiding there too, and slug eggs. These can be conveniently collected and destroyed.

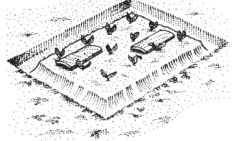

◆ SLUG PREDATORS AND PARASITES ◆

As slugs do not normally die of starvation, there must be something that naturally prevents them from eating every green plant in sight – after all, one grey field slug could potentially have 90,000 grandchildren and 27,000,000 great grandchildren if all were to survive. There are three main (non-human) causes of death for slugs: weather, diseases and predators.

A number of creepy-crawlies will eat them. These range from rare beauties like glow worms and their larvae to common centipedes. Many species of ground beetles (known as carabids) will eat slugs. These are the fast-running black beetles, found in almost all gardens. Although they will occasionally nibble a strawberry for moisture during dry weather, they otherwise do nothing but good. When not eating slugs, they will be tackling other soft-bodied pests, such as caterpillars and aphids. The devil's coach horses and related staphilinid beetles eat slugs too and are common in gardens, although less often seen.

Carabid beetle

Then there are the testacella slugs. These extraordinary creatures, found mainly in southern counties, are only distantly related to other slugs. They are carnivorous, almost entirely subterranean, have a small shell on their backs and are not slimy. They are frequently found in deep leaf mould and organically rich soil. The three species native to Britain, up to 4½ inches (12 cm) long, orange in colour from pale cream to grey/brown with a yellow or orange sole and characteristic veining along the sides of the body. They pursue worms and burrowing slugs underground. Not only do they do no harm, these are slugs that do good too.

The most important parasites of slugs are the marsh flies (sciomyzids). The females lay 300 eggs or more, and each developing larva will kill several slugs, especially grey field slugs. Although called marsh flies, these insects are not confined to wet areas and can be found wherever there are slugs. You have to be an expert to identify them as they are simply anonymous-looking flies, about ¼ inch (6 mm) long, but it is very good to know that they are there.

Reptiles and amphibians may not be overwhelmingly popular, but they will do no harm to you or your plants and include several slug eaters. Frogs are the best, the most common and the most easily encouraged. They prefer damp sites, where slugs abound, and hunt by ambushing anything edible that passes. A quarter of their diet frequently comprises slugs. Toads and slow worms eat slugs too and can be helpful in drier parts of the garden, particularly rockeries.

Many mammals eat slugs, including badgers and foxes, but the best known slug-eating mammal must be the hedgehog. This creature forages at night, 'hoovering' up worms and slugs, particularly on lawns; unfortunately, like birds and amphibians, it will take ground beetles too. It is to be hoped that the beetles are more successful at escaping than the slugs, and that on balance hedgehogs are doing more good than harm. I am inclined to give them the benefit of the doubt.

Birds are the most important of the larger predators. The long list of species known to eat slugs includes blackbirds and thrushes, robins, starlings, rooks and crows, magpies, jays, ducks, seagulls and even owls! Song thrushes are well known for snail eating. If you find a stone or paving slab with a scattering of broken snail shells around it, you know that either a song thrush or a redwing has been at work. The stone is used as an anvil to break the shell. These birds frequently eat slugs in even greater quantity, but there are no tell-tale remains to prove it.

Encouraging Predators

Encouraging predators is an enormous subject and involves adopting many of the techniques advocated for creating a wildlife garden. You do not, however, have to go the whole hog, but can select elements that fit in with your personal gardening philosophy and encourage the best slug predators at the same time.

For example, if you use pesticides, such as slug pellets, you can minimise the dangers to insects and birds by protecting the treated site with netting, and clearing away the poisons afterwards, as suggested earlier (page 34). Controlled refuges (page 39) will then provide sites in which beetles can exist in the tidiest of beds.

British gardeners tend to favour the type of plantings that create a suitable environment for predators in any case, with dense shrubberies and hedges to provide shelter, food and nesting sites for birds, and herbaceous borders that encourage many insect predators. Thrushes and starlings survive the winter by eating fruits and berries, so many of our favourite shrubs and trees, including rowan, holly, berberis, cotoneaster and crab apple, will help to persuade them to stay. Ponds are excellent, particularly with attached bog gardens. These will provide breeding and feeding sites for frogs and toads, although large fish must not be kept as they eat the tadpoles. The water will be appreciated by birds, for bathing and drinking, and with associated flowers will attract marsh flies. Nestboxes will attract more birds, particularly starlings, which will also eat the dreaded leatherjackets and other pests. They may be 'greedy' birds, but that is exactly what you want in a pest controller! Nestboxes can also be made for hedgehogs. These consist of a strong box, approximately 20 inches (50 cm) square, with an entrance tunnel and a ventilation pipe, that can be buried in soil or under leaf mould. Hedgehogs can then hibernate there, undisturbed and safe, ready to breed more slug hunters the following spring.

You can, where appropriate, introduce your own bird predators in the form of ducks or chickens. Hens are very destructive unless confined, but if moved over vacant ground in an ark or fold, they will not only clear the weeds, fertilise the ground and provide you with eggs, but also eat any slugs and other pests that they come upon. Ducks, on the other hand, do far less damage to crops, and have been used in the Far East for centuries to clear snails from rice fields. There they are trained to go to a flag set in the crop and clear snails in the vicinity. If given plenty of space, and an area of grass to graze, they will not do much harm to cultivated plants, although seedlings need protection from their big feet!

Beetles can be concentrated in beds containing vulnerable plants by the construction of pitfall barriers (Fig. 2). These consist of a surrounding wall of smooth, corrugated lawn edging, constructed so that the soil outside the plot is flush with the top of the wall, while the soil inside is at least 1¼ inches (3 cm) below the top of the same wall. The idea is that beetles running around the garden at night fall in and are trapped inside the bed. The smooth wall then prevents them from climbing out, and as most cannot fly, this results in a rapid increase in the density of beetles on the site. It is important to provide them with shelter, so 'controlled refuges' must be used. To get a good catch the outside soil must be precisely flush with the top of the wall, and sand can be used to help achieve this. The sand will also help deter invading slugs. Be sure to allow the beetles out again when the crop is cleared, because they will be needed again and must be allowed to find suitable breeding sites in the garden.

◆ RESISTANT PLANT VARIETIES ◆

Slug-resistant varieties of vegetables and ornamentals exist and can make an important contribution to reductions in damage. It must be added, however, that the potential for this has been little explored, and it is an example of an area of research that requires more support. Resistance is a very satisfying method of slug control, involving no work or side effects, and no additional costs. It is certainly worth taking the extra trouble to choose suitable varieties.

But do not imagine that resistance implies immunity – no potato is immune to keel slug attack, for example. Nevertheless, damage to potatoes is certainly greater in some varieties than others, and the list below divides cultivars into three categories.

VULNERABILITY OF POTATO VARIETIES TO SLUG ATTACK		
High Resistance	**Intermediate**	**Low Resistance**
'Pentland Dell'	'Majestic'	'Maris Piper'
'Pentland Ivory'	'Desirée'	'Cara'
'Pentland Falcon'	'King Edward'	'Kingston'
	'Pentland Crown'	'Ulster Glade'
	'Pentland Hawk'	
	'Record'	
	'Romano'	

Brassicas too have different levels of resistance according to type. In general, greater resistance can be found in spring cabbage, kale and sprouting broccoli, while summer cabbage, savoy, cauliflower and Brussels sprouts are more susceptible. It is often the sweeter, more succulent varieties that we, and the slugs, like best. I love the F1 'Hispi' cabbage raw in salads; the slugs love it raw in the garden and seem to appear out of nowhere just as the plants approach maturity. It is the same with lettuces: the sweeter they are, the more attractive they appear to be to slugs. When they taste of chicory or dandelion, they have more resistance. Such bitter-tasting elements in the leaves are often chemicals produced by the plant to deter pests. We breed out the bitterness, and should not be surprised that pest problems are correspondingly intensified.

What a slug chooses depends upon what is on offer. When I presented slugs with both chrysanthemums and lettuces, they all chose the lettuces. And yet slugs are major pests of commercially-grown chrysanthemums. So, if you grow these flowers try putting a few lettuces in among them as a sacrificial crop to attract the slugs away. The slugs can thus be localised and dealt with while on the lettuces. Alternatively, or in addition, you can choose resistant varieties.

Lilies come from different wild ancestors and have inherited varying degrees of ancestral resistance due to hybridisation. The roots of *Lilium davidii* and *Lilium regale* are attacked by keel slugs, while those of *Lilium henryi* and *Lilium tigrinum* are rarely affected.

Most hosta growers know that varieties with blue leaves have greater resistance to slugs than those with yellowish or variegated leaves. In this case a chemical that contributes to the colour, or one inherited with the blue colour, is effectively deterring slugs from attacking.

As new plant varieties appear regularly, you must simply be alert to any differences you notice in the garden. You might do better to replace with a more resistant alternative any variety that attracts slugs like a magnet rather than attempting to engage in a prolonged battle of attrition with the slugs.

◆ INTEGRATED CONTROL ◆

The practical gardener might well say that you should not only use chemicals sparingly in the garden, but that you should also spend money sparingly too! To this I fully subscribe. However, it is important to take hidden cost into your accounting. Pellets may be cheap, but if they cause the death of slug predators, the 'second wave' of slugs might well be worse than the first and be more costly to control and in terms of vegetables lost. The same principle applies to the time you spend: a method that is quick and easy in the short term might well cause you more work and trouble in the end. This does not mean that you should never use chemicals. It simply means that, when you do, use them when and where they will do greatest harm to the slugs, but the least to the predators.

Practical slug control will always be a matter of combining methods according to circumstances. You cannot use a rotovator in a rockery, or use pellets if you keep pigeons, or use a slug-resistant variety of a particular plant if it is not obtainable or if you do not like it! Preserving slug predators has long-term benefits and reduces the need for emergency action when pellets may be the only answer. Correct timing can avoid trouble too. For instance, lifting potatoes earlier than usual will avoid the period of greatest slug damage in autumn. It is at this time when slugs are at their most numerous and the potatoes are most attractive to them because the surface haulms, on which slugs feed, will have died off and the slugs burrow down for their food, avoiding the cooler conditions on the surface.

Use of a rotovator, as described on page 39, will clear large numbers of slugs in spring. If this is followed by the use of a contact spray (metaldehyde or aluminium sulphate, for example) the same evening, when slugs are very active, seeking new food sources and refuges, their increased activity will result in increased contact with the poison and a high percentage of those remaining will be destroyed. Having thus reduced the population of slugs considerably, you will find that further measures (controlled refuges, beer traps, barriers and so on) will be that much more effective.

◆ NEW DEVELOPMENTS ◆

Not much seems to have changed in slug control in the last twenty years. Fortunately, this state of affairs is about to alter dramatically. Some of the new developments are outlined below.

Low-dose pellets have been created, containing a detergent-like sub-stance which increases the rate at which the metaldehyde content is absorbed by the slug's skin or gut. This allows pellets with only half the usual amount of metaldehyde to be as effective at killing slugs as conventional pellets, with obvious environmental benefits. Another new pellet, soon to be marketed, uses a chemical identical to that found in the ragworm (as used by fishermen) as part of this creature's defences; it might thus be classed as an organic slug pellet. A further natural slug killer is found in a plant from Africa called endod or soap berry (*Phytolacca dodecandra*). The crushed berries are used by natives for washing. It was discovered that in lakes and rivers where this natural soap was used, all the snails died. The related *Phytolacca americana* has similar properties and is a temperate plant, so perhaps one day you will be able to grow your own slug killer.

Strains of the now familiar *Bacillus thuringiensis*, used to control caterpillars, may be adapted to a slug-killing role, and the power of other newly discovered natural micro-organisms may be harnessed to this effect too. If these worked, they would provide a simple spray-on treatment that would be harmless to everything except slugs.

My own work with beetles has revealed the existence of one species, *Abax parallelepipedus*, which has a proven ability to clear slugs from a crop. This beetle could be mass-produced and made available to gardeners and growers in pupa form. When the pupae hatch, they could be introduced to infested crops, surrounded by plastic walls to prevent the beetles from escaping. The beetles are easily managed (they cannot fly), are harmless to people and plants, and should they escape they would in many cases simply join natural populations. *Abax* is particularly effective against the grey field slug.

◆ CONCLUSION ◆

If you have read this far, you will at least have discovered that there is more to slug control than a packet of pellets. And, please, don't panic: there are options here for all situations, and new solutions on the horizon.

For further information:

A *Field Guide to the Slugs of the British Isles* by R. A. D. Cameron, N. Jackson and B. Eversham (Field Studies Series, Invicta Press).
and A *Field Guide to the Land Snails of Britain and North-West Europe* by M. P. Kerney and R. A. D. Cameron (Collins) are both very useful.

◆ HERBS ◆

by John Kelly

To hear people talk, you would think that the world had only just woken up to herbs. Suddenly they are not just popular, but positively fashionable, and everyone knows that anything in fashion is also in peril. It would be a great shame if the current surge of interest were to be a mere blip in their extremely long history; perhaps the antidote to the kiss of death that fashion bestows will be a genuine and lasting return to values that have been temporarily sunk beneath the tidal wave of modern industrial culture.

The true value of herbs to mankind has been hidden from most of us by our own perverse inclination to erect academic superstructures on bodies of traditional knowledge. You can see this happening among those gardeners whose eye for beauty has been obliterated by their desire to be more and more deeply involved with Latin and botanical minutiae. The herbalists, recoiling from being mere tradesmen, sought to create a profession, and in so doing devised nonsenses like the Doctrine of Signatures, in which a plant, fancifully supposed to look like lung tissue, would be used to treat respiratory ailments and another, in some tortuous way deemed to appear bloodshot, found itself prized for the treatment of eyes.

What is so encouraging about today's interest is that the wheel has come full circle, and modern scientific thinking, limpidly accurate where seventeenth-century speculation was messy, has taken the study and use of herbs forward in a way that has not been seen since the fall of the Roman Empire.

It is not often realised how very new modern botanical knowledge is. Dioscorides, a Greek living in the first century AD, wrote a book on medicinal herbs that was regarded almost as holy writ until the modern era. Indeed, 'holy' is not too far off the mark; Gerard, whose largely plagiarised herbal dates from the time of James I, refers to him as 'divine'. What a satisfying coincidence it is that the contraceptive pill, that most secular of humanity's recent advances, should have been first prepared from the root of a species of *Dioscorea*, the genus named in his honour.

What the ancient Greeks and the Renaissance herbalists had in common with modern doctors was a realistic knowledge of the power of herbs. You do not play about with substances that can save life in small doses but kill in larger ones, especially when the line to be drawn is a fine one. Foxgloves contain active principles that can revive a flagging heart, but can also stop a healthy one forever. *Rauwolfia serpentina*, the Indian snake-root, provides a means of lowering blood pressure and was the basis of the introduction of tranquillisers but it, and *Veratrum viride*, whose actions are similar, are deadly poisons as well.

Gardeners should never dabble in the medicinal uses of herbs. That is not to say that they should not consult properly qualified people – far from it – but as one of the few professional gardeners to have also worked in the pharmaceutical industry I feel justified in saying that a fascination with the plants is one thing; to be tempted to use them is another.

A legitimate interest in herbs is most likely to begin with the discovery of those that are used in the kitchen. Like so many interests, however, it soon develops into a hobby and the herb element of the garden increases rapidly. One aspect of this is that a certain apparent weediness creeps in, but it is only apparent, as many plants that we think of as weeds are, in fact, herbs.

So what is a herb? The best answer is probably that it is a plant that has a use to mankind other than as food. In other words, if you grow horseradish to make into a sauce for beef, it is a food. Grow it to put on rheumatic joints and it is a herb. Lettuce, on the other hand, is a food plant in its cultivated form, but the wild lettuce (*Lactuca virosa*) is a powerful and potentially dangerous herb with strong sedative qualities.

A gardener who wished to grow wild lettuce might well include shepherd's purse among acceptable garden plants, whereas you and I would question the presence of such an obvious weed. Its weediness is, in fact, open to debate, and we should remember that a weed is merely a plant that is in the wrong place. In gardens it is the gardener who is to be the judge of that, not the observer.

If a gardener wishes to grow shepherd's purse, I am entitled to think that he is a nut case if I wish. I may also ask him, if his plantation gets out of hand and infects my garden with its seed, to restrict its numbers to an acceptable level. What I must not do is to say that he is wrong. Apart from anything else, we are, as long as we behave reasonably, at liberty to grow just what we like – short of weeds, like ragwort, that are classified as pernicious; and *Cannabis indica*. In addition, though, there is the grave danger of my making an ass of myself by not heeding Emerson, who declared that a weed was 'a plant whose virtues have not yet been discovered'.

It would serve me right, then, if I were to be told firmly that shepherd's purse contains the chemical that permits our nerves to transmit messages to our muscles; that it is good for stopping bleeding, for haemorrhoids, and for varicose veins, and that I should swiftly depart hence – or words to that effect.

As I am, however, addressing gardeners and not the more extreme collectors of herbs (nut cases?), I will not advocate the assiduous cultivation of dandelions, horsetail, yellow dock or common plantain. I will stick to plants that are decorative and have uses that are relevant to everyday life. For example, you might like to know that lemon verbena makes a nice tea that is good for indigestion, but you would not thank me for advocating the thorn apple *(Datura stramonium)*, which admittedly has a use in asthma, but which is subject to the Poisons Act and easily causes palpitation, hallucination and an unrelievable desire to urinate. On top of that, it is a very ugly plant.

♦ CULINARY HERBS ♦

The herb garden – if there is to be such a thing and you are not dotting herbs among the general planting – should be in a position where the plants will be happiest. In practice it will not be all that often that you suddenly remember the salad burnet in the middle of a thunderstorm. Anyway, most gardens are small and it takes only a moment to reach their further corners.

There is not a lot of gardening attached to growing culinary herbs. There is no cause to fret about acid and alkaline soils, no need further to deplete the finite peat stocks of the world, and you can, if you like, indulge in a freedom from the Latin names that I like, but which probably annoy you no end. It is good to use names like chervil, descended through Old English and Latin from the ancient Greek for 'leaf of gladness', or to share with Shakespeare the Englishness of thyme.

About two thirds of culinary herbs die down to soil level or below for the winter, so you have to be a bit adroit if you are going to get the most out of them. The use of cloches is likely to extend the herb season by weeks rather than days, and some, such as chives, mints and marjoram, will carry on through the winter if they are potted up and brought inside.

The reminder that culinary herb plants tend to come from places with hot summers may serve to warn us that the corollary may be a dislike of very cold winters. Hyssop and rosemary, which are shrubs, are hardier than lemon verbena and bay, but it is a good idea to give them protection in really bad winters, using straw, hay, hessian or fine-mesh garden netting.

These are perennial plants, in the sense that they live for a number of years. Others may be annual or biennial or, like chervil and parsley, biennial but best treated as annual. With the exception of parsley, which is usually extremely slow to germinate (though it is sometimes perverse and comes up straight away), the annuals are easy from seed, which can be sown either outdoors in drills or in pots under cover.

It is a very good practice to take cuttings of perennial herbs. This is not just in case the plants are lost in a cold winter (although this is a most important reason), but also because the best growth for kitchen use is obtained from young plants that are growing vigorously. The material will in general be softer and less fibrous, more likely to surrender its full flavour and to be more subtle to the taste. Nodal  cuttings are usually best – I tend to take French tarragon with a heel (*right*), but I don't think it is essential – and rooting is usually quick and sure if the cuttings are half-ripe in the case of shrubby plants or soft in the case of herbaceous ones. Shrubby plants with tiny leaves, like ordinary and lemon thyme, root best from soft cuttings taken in spring.

If division is used as a method of propagation, it is even more important than with other plants that the old, central crowns should be thrown away and only the young, outer ones re-planted. Don't give them away, either: you won't be doing anyone a favour.

You might think that, because the young growths of herbs are the best, it would be a good idea to manure them heavily to get them to grow fast and make even more young growth. This is not a good idea, as their original hot homes tended to be stony places with poor soil. Too rich a diet will make them grow out of character and, what is more, their aromatic content will decline, leading to insipidness and much-reduced culinary value.

Herbs contain all sorts of complex chemicals, some of which are beneficial or harmless to us, but unpleasant or lethal to pests. This applies more to medicinal herbs, but it is nevertheless part of the reason why culinary herbs suffer very little from attack. It is a very bad thing to go in for indiscriminate spraying around food plants of any kind; with herbs it is not necessary.

◆ SOME HERBS FOR KITCHEN USE ◆

BALM, LEMON
(Melissa officinalis)

Hardy herbaceous perennial. New shoots appear in spring, growing to form heart-shaped leaves, which are strongly lemon-scented. Used in drinks, salads, omelettes; also with fish and cottage cheese.

In the garden does not like to become too dry. Propagate by division in autumn or seed in spring.

The name *Melissa* refers to its attractiveness to bees: it is an excellent honey plant. It has been used in medicine for feverish colds and 'flu and contains citronella oil, which is sedative. It was once an ingredient of furniture polish.

BASIL
(Ocimum basilicum)

A half-hardy annual with white flowers in summer. Used mainly in Mediterranean cooking, and in a starter dish with olive oil and tomatoes in France. Its flavour is strong, so it should be used sparingly.

Germinates quickly if sown in gentle heat in early spring, or outdoors in late spring. Pinch out. Pot up in autumn for winter use.

BAY
(Laurus nobilis)

A shrub or small tree. Can be clipped to shape and grown as a standard if desired. Best grown in a container away from the south and west, and brought indoors for winter. Used in many kinds of cooking – in soups, casseroles, birianis and so on. Also used in *bouquets garnis*.

Can be grown from the black berries, but germination may take two years.

Also known as laurel. The laurel wreaths of the Romans were of bay. Graduating students, having been bound to chastity during their studies, were crowned with bay and were dubbed *bacca lauriae* – laurel berries. From this comes 'bachelor' for an unmarried man or a university graduate.

The cherry laurel *(Prunus laurocerasus)*, often also known simply as laurel, must not be confused with *Laurus nobilis*, as it is highly poisonous.

BORAGE
(Borago officinalis)

A hardy annual up to 3 ft (90 cm) tall. Large, roughly hairy leaves with brilliant, forget-me-not blue flowers all summer. A fine garden plant for mixing with others in the general border.

The leaves and particularly the flowers are used to flavour drinks, especially the sort that are sipped by young, upwardly mobile people at 'dos' on lawns. Not the most vital of herbs for home use.

Sow outdoors in mid-spring.

Borage has been widely and effectively used for centuries as a medicinal herb and has recently been recognised as a major source of an important principle for the treatment of rheumatoid arthritis. Unfortunately for those who tried to grow it commercially for the purpose, waste pulp from blackcurrants was found to contain more.

CHERVIL
(Anthriscus cerefolium)

A hardy biennial, best grown as an annual. Ferny leaves on quite a small – 1 ft (30 cm) – plant. It has a distinct aniseed flavour. It is not widely used in Britain, but should be, as it is excellent in salads, with fish and in *omelette fines herbes*.

Successional sowings every month or so in a good moisture-retentive soil will provide leaves for use from spring to autumn. It reacts well to cloche cultivation. It is a major herb in French cookery; in Britain its last burst of popularity was among Elizabethans, who used it to freshen the skin from within when the application of soap and water without would have been more effective.

CHIVES
(Allium schoenoprasum)

A bulbous plant, making a dense cluster of tubular leaves like those of a small onion. It bears round heads of purple-blue flowers in summer and dies down in autumn.

Chives are used in many ways in the kitchen. The leaves are generally finely chopped, but in Denmark they are often used whole. Soups and salads, as well as many cooked dishes, benefit from the addition of chives, and several kinds of cheese are made with them. The Chinese used chives at least five thousand years ago and still do. The plant reached us by the agency of the Romans.

DILL
(Anethum graveolens)

A hardy annual, rather similar in appearance to fennel, dill is used with fish and in salads. The seeds are bitter to the taste but are an excellent ingredient in pickling liquors.

It should be sown outdoors in early spring if it is not still cold. It should not be transplanted, but sown where it is to grow and then thinned. A summer sowing will provide plants for autumn.

Dill is one of the few herbs whose medicinal value may be exploited without harm by amateurs, as oil of dill is good for the digestion. It is used in gripe waters for children.

FENNEL
(Foeniculum vulgare)

Fennel is a hardy perennial with feathery, ferny leaves, very finely cut, and umbels of yellow flowers in summer; Florence fennel differs in that it has a bulbous root rather than a carrot-like one. It finds its main use in fish cookery, where its distinctive flavour, whose nearest ally is probably chervil, is of great value. It is also used in sauces and soups. The root of Florence fennel is boiled as a vegetable.

Propagation is by seed sown outdoors in mid-spring. Fennel must have a well-drained soil; if it fails to reappear in spring this is usually because of wet rather than cold.

Medicinally it is used as a tea to counter indigestion and it is said to help weight reduction by inducing a lack of hunger. An eyebath prepared from fennel is held to be most soothing.

LEMON-SCENTED VERBENA
(Lippia citriodora)

A shrub, suitable for the mild parts of Britain, or as a tub or conservatory plant elsewhere. Usually about 3 ft (90 cm) high, it bears lilac flowers in summer. It is strongly and pleasantly lemon-scented. Lemon verbena is used in stuffings and a very pleasant tea is made from it which is good for the digestion.

Keep going from cuttings. It can become untidy and leggy, so needs to be pruned back a little, especially if it is pot-grown.

LOVAGE
(Levisticum officinale)

Lovage is a big, ugly member of the fennel family, growing to over 6 ft (2 m) tall and with untidy, pinnate leaves. It is a perennial.

Its taste in cooking is sometimes described as yeasty, and sometimes as celery-like. I find it unpleasant, but it is much prized for use in soups and casseroles and with fish.

Lovage can be raised from seed or propagated from root cuttings taken in early spring. It should be tidied up for the winter as soon as is decent.

THE MARJORAMS
(*Origanum* species)

O. *marjorana* is sweet marjoram, O. *vulgare* is wild marjoram (or oregano) and O. *onites* is the pot marjoram that is used in winter. The first two are annual, while the third is perennial, but not nearly as well-flavoured. Sweet marjoram is used widely with meat, as a sausage flavouring and with vegetables. Oregano finds a wide use wherever pizza is made, and is excellent with meat and in quiches and other egg dishes. Pot marjoram is used only in cold parts of the world where sweet marjoram is made an annual by cold winters.

Sweet marjoram is sown where it is to grow in mid-spring and then thinned to 1 ft (30 cm) apart. Oregano can be raised in similar fashion or from cuttings.

THE MINTS
(*Mentha* species)

Hardy perennials with invasive roots. M. *spicata* is the common mint, M. *rotundifolia* is apple mint, M. *aquatica* is water mint. M. *piperita* is peppermint, and is a flavouring rather than a herb.

Common mint is, of course, used with meat, especially lamb, and can be obtained for the table as a particularly revolting green jelly.

Cultivation is a matter of containment, and it is best grown in a sunken bucket whose bottom has been removed.

Peppermint contains menthol and has many medicinal uses. The old herbalists recommended its application to bites from mad dogs: a case of giving hope where no hope lay!

ROSEMARY
(*Rosmarinus officinalis*)

An evergreen shrub, hardy in all but the coldest winters, growing to about 3 ft (90 cm). The most attractive form is 'Miss Jessup's Upright', with an erect habit, narrow leaves and many flowers in spring. Rosemary is unmistakable in its flavour and is used with meat, especially lamb and pork.

It requires a dry, sunny place and can be grown from soft cuttings in spring or semi-ripe ones in summer.

Before Ancient Greek students graduated and were crowned with bay leaves, they wound rosemary in their hair to aid concentration. Perhaps they then applied catmint – still used to combat baldness.

SAGE
(Salvia officinalis)

An evergreen shrub, the hardiest of its genus and hardy in Britain if the soil is not waterlogged in winter. Sage is used with pork, duck and any other fatty meat which needs a touch of astringency. With onion it makes a delicious stuffing. Sage tea is highly esteemed by some; to me it is suggestive of an infusion of old socks.

Sage does not mean 'wise', but comes from the Latin for 'to save'. It was regarded as a cure for almost anything. If it was drunk as a tea, it was supposed to make you forget any ailment – and I can well believe this!

TARRAGON
(Artemisia dracunculus)

A perennial plant, evergreen in mild winters and not more than 2 ft (60 cm) tall. It is advisable to obtain French tarragon, as its flavour is the best.

Tarragon is used much more in Britain than hitherto; it is one of the herbs that the French have used for a long time without its crossing the Channel. It is a superb assistance to chicken, is an ingredient of *omelette fines herbes* and is used to make tarragon vinegar.

Tarragon needs shelter from the worst winter weather and should not be grown in soils that lie wet.

Henry VIII would allow tarragon to be grown only in the royal gardens. The name does not derive from that of one of his wives but from *estragon* (a small dragon), the Latin for which is the specific epithet *dracunculus*.

THYME
(Thymus serpyllum)

Common thyme is a tiny, creeping shrub, no more than a few inches high. It is hardy, as is *T. citriodorus*, the lemon thyme.

Thyme is used widely with meat and poultry, and is an ingredient of stuffings, particularly in combination with parsley. Lemon thyme is used by some people in fish dishes, but I prefer to use lemon juice and grow the plant for its ornamental value.

Thyme likes a sunny spot in paving or the rock garden. Spring cuttings are fiddly, but root well.

The plant has wide medical use. One of its oils, thymol, is an ingredient of many expectorant cough mixtures and is used in tropical countries as an anti-parasitic. Thyme is good for the digestion if drunk as a tea. This applies to many herbs; personally I would suffer the indigestion.

◆ PRUNING ◆

by Geoff Hamilton

There's more myth and mystery, worry and heartache over pruning than just about any other job in the garden. I have a theory that the old head gardeners used to exaggerate the difficulty of many gardening tasks in order to ensure their superiority over their staff. And that legacy of mystique has been handed down through generations of gardeners so that now we're all terrified to raise a pair of secateurs.

In fact, there's very little to worry about because it's actually extremely difficult to kill most plants by cutting bits off them. The majority will reply by growing even stronger. It all becomes quite simple when you start to look at *why* we prune.

◆ REASONS FOR PRUNING ◆

Tidying

The first job when you're pruning anything at all is to look for dead wood and cut it out. There's no need to do so, but it makes the plant look tidier and it removes a potential source of disease. When doing this, cut beyond the dead wood into live wood, cutting just above a bud (*near right*). The reason for always pruning just above a bud is that this is where the healing chemicals are concentrated. If you leave a stub (*far right*), the wood will simply die back to just above the bud anyway.

Thinning

Sometimes, trees and shrubs get very congested, with a mass of thin, weak shoots all fighting each other for light and air. The plant will look and feel better and produce better flowers and fruit if some of that tangle is removed. But think about it long *before* the plant becomes a mess.

As a general rule of thumb, check all your woody plants – shrubs, trees, roses and fruit trees – in the autumn or early spring and remove any branches that are very weak and any that are growing into the centre of the bush instead of outwards, or are crossing others.

Invigorating

Occasionally, if plants are getting on in years, it pays to cut out some of the older shoots to encourage new, young, vigorous ones. Again, don't leave it too long or you'll find yourself cutting away half the plant. The way to do it is to cut back either right down to the ground or back to a strong side shoot coming from low down on the bush (*below*). Some, like hypericums for example, can be sheared off right down to the ground in autumn or early spring and they'll thrive, producing a mass of new shoots from the base. This technique is often used to remove fungus diseases like hypericum rust completely. When you prune in this way, it's best to feed as well, using a rose fertiliser for all woody plants, including shrubs and fruit trees.

Encouraging

Often plants can be encouraged to produce better flowers and fruit and more of them by pruning. This is usually done in the summer when, as a rule, plants respond by making flower instead of growth buds.

Shaping

Sometimes you can control the size and shape of a tree or shrub by judicious pruning. But here you have to be careful. If you simply cut off the ends of the branches of many plants, they'll respond by growing two, three or even more shoots from the cut. So your plant begins to look like a moulting lavatory brush! While it is possible to trim some plants like this – potentillas are a good example – it's generally better to cut back complete shoots to the point where they join a larger branch (*right*).

When you do this job, take a lot of time and stand back and eye up the plant often, judging whether or not you can afford to remove a little more. It's easy to cut bits off but not to stick them back on again!

Maintaining

Sometimes plants grow suckers from their roots which are not the same as the variety which is grafted on to them. These must be removed before they take over, because they're likely to be much more vigorous than the variety.

Likewise, some variegated plants revert and produce green shoots. Again, cut them right out.

Trimming

Some plants are pruned simply by cutting off a proportion of the new shoots with shears. Hedges or topiary are the obvious examples. But even here a little care is needed, especially with conifers. Many will not re-shoot from the old wood, so if you cut off all the new growth you'll be left with old, brown, leafless shoots and your hedge will be ruined. For this reason you *must* trim the sides of new hedges, especially conifers, as soon as they get to the required width. Leave the tops until they've got to the right height before cutting back.

• SHRUBS •

By no means all flowering shrubs need pruning to encourage healthy growth and good flowering. Some, like rhododendrons and camellias, will go on flowering year after year without ever seeing a pair of secateurs. Others need pruning every year to obtain the best results.

Deciduous shrubs (those which lose their leaves in winter) can conveniently be divided into three groups.

1 Those that flower in spring or early summer
This group includes shrubs like forsythia, deutzia, flowering currant, kerria, weigela and philadelphus. They flower on wood made the previous season; so, in order to give the plant the maximum amount of time to produce long, flowering shoots, pruning should be done immediately after flowering. The received wisdom is that all the shoots that have just flowered should be removed completely. However, my own experience has been that this often results in a mass of long, strong shoots which grow out very vigorously but don't flower. On plants like forsythia it's often the short, twiggy side shoots arising from older wood that bear the most flowers. Therefore, rather than cutting the whole plant down every year, I would prefer to cut out no more than half the new wood immediately after flowering. Cut the shoots right out to the base if possible, or to a joint with another branch low down on the bush. Make sure you feed with a rose fertiliser afterwards.

2 Those that flower in late summer or autumn, bearing their flowers on the tips of the growth they made in the same season
Shrubs in this group include the butterfly bush (*Buddleia davidii*), fuchsias and deciduous ceanothus. It's best to wait until early spring to prune them because then you'll be able to see swelling buds. Cut back hard to leave just a short length of the old stem, no more than a couple of inches long (*see opposite*). Again, it's as well to feed simultaneously to boost the shoots as they grow out very rapidly to make ample growth by flowering time.

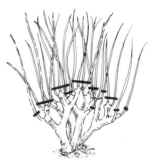

Indeed, it's possible to delay flowering a little by cutting back late – say, in late April or even May. This is sometimes a good practice with buddleia, since it will then provide a late feed for butterflies.

Some smaller shrubs like hypericums can be cut right back to the ground from time to time to encourage strong, bushy, new growth.

3 Those grown for their foliage or colour of bark

This group includes such foliage plants as the variegated weigela (*Weigela florida* 'Variegata'), the variegated dogwoods (*Cornus alba* varieties) and the smoke tree (*Cotinus coggygria*). If the shoots are cut back quite hard in March or early April, the size of the leaves will be greatly increased. Others, like some of the spiraeas (notably the newer foliage types like 'Goldflame' and 'Golden Princess'), will produce more vivid foliage if they are cut back hard in early spring.

Those grown for their bark, like many of the coloured willows, dogwoods and brambles, will produce their most vibrant colours if the shoots are cut back hard either to the ground or to a basic framework of older branches each spring.

Evergreen shrubs can often be left alone, but there are a few exceptions. Some plants, like artemisias and santolina, tend to get very straggly after a while. When this happens they can be cut back very hard. They'll soon shoot out again to make a compact bush. The same thing happens to plants like lavender, but these won't shoot out from old wood. The only way here is to avoid their becoming straggly by cutting back with a pair of shears immediately after flowering or in early spring.

◆ TREES ◆

Many garden-centre trees are sold as 'feathered' specimens these days. That means that, instead of a traditional shape with a bare trunk carrying a 'crown' of branches on top, the tree consists of a central stem with branches arising from it all the way down.

Some gardeners prefer to grow their trees in this shape, when they will make what amounts to a large shrub. However, if you want the traditional shape, you'll have to prune them yourself.

To do so, wait until the tree has grown about 1 ft (30 cm) taller than the point at which you wish to start the crown. When it has, cut back to the required height in the winter. This will result in four or five branches growing out from the pruning point. Allow them to grow out in the first year and, when they are growing well and thickening up, cut off the remaining shoots below the crown close to the trunk. Then it's just a case of keeping an eye on the tree and removing any branches that grow in towards the middle of the crown or any that are crossing or overcrowded.

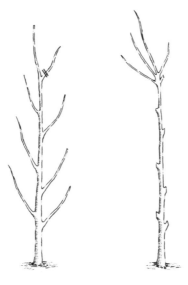

Cut to the required height in winter (left) and remove remaining shoots the next summer (right)

The exceptions to the winter pruning rule are the flowering cherries, almonds, peaches and plums. Like their fruiting cousins, they're best pruned when they start into growth in the spring. They are subject to the fungus disease silver leaf which can enter through wounds, so it's best to prune at a time when the trees are growing quickly and will rapidly heal.

◆ CLIMBERS ◆

Self-clinging climbers like Virginia creeper, hydrangeas and ivy really need no pruning short of removing shoots that are growing where they're not wanted. I once returned from holiday to find that a Virginia creeper had wormed its way through a crack in the front door and was twined round the telephone in the hall! A trim over with shears can be used to tidy up from time to time if necessary.

To encourage the flowering of wisteria and vines, it's often recommended that a basic framework is first built up and then the side growths be shortened to short 'spurs' in August or September. That's good advice in the early years but later, when the plant covers the side of the house, it's a little unrealistic. If you can manage it, however, and couple it with feeding, it'll certainly encourage flowering.

Vigorous twiners like honeysuckle will also need containing; do this simply by hacking off bits that have grown where they shouldn't.

Judging by the letters we get at *Gardeners' World*, one of the biggest headaches of all is clematis. It needn't be – provided you remember its name, or at least what type it is, and when it flowers. The vigorous species like *Clematis montana*, *C. macropetala*, *C. chrysocoma* and *C. alpina* simply need cutting back where they get out of control. This is best done as they finish flowering by cutting back to the main framework of older shoots.

The large-flowered hybrids are divided into two groups. Those that flower early (from early May to the end of June) produce their flowers on last season's wood. If you look closely at these plants in February, you'll see a number of strong buds about to burst out from this older wood. Cut back to the highest pair of strong buds, shortening the growths by about 1 ft (30 cm) or so. This group includes varieties like 'Bees Jubilee', 'Duchess of Edinburgh', 'Ernest Markham', 'Barbara Jackman', 'Henryi', 'Jackmanii Alba', 'Lasurstern', 'Mrs Cholmondeley', 'Nelly Moser', 'Niobe', 'Richard Pennell', 'The President', 'Vyvyan Pennell' and 'William Kennett'.

The third group produce all their flowers on the wood made in the same season, and they are the late flowerers – from July onwards. These are best cut back hard each year: remove all growth to a point about 2–3 ft (60 cm–1 m) above the ground. This group includes 'Comtesse de Bouchaud', 'Ernest Markham', 'Jackmanii Superba', 'Lady Betty Balfour', *C. orientalis*, *C. tangutica*, 'Ville de Lyon' and *C. viticella*.

◆ *ROSES* ◆

I have to admit to being a bit of a butcher where bush roses are concerned. My experience has been that a good hard pruning each year, coupled with a feed, will produce healthy, strong growth and better blooms. When pruning, cut back to an outward- or downward-facing bud, cutting just above the bud without leaving a long snag.

New roses planted in autumn or early spring should be pruned really hard, leaving only about two or three buds per shoot. Weak shoots can be removed completely. Naturally, if you're planting container-grown roses during the summer, the pruning should wait until March, but then hard treatment is still the order of the day.

Subsequently, prune in March, cutting back HT (hybrid tea) roses to leave strong stems about 3 inches (7.5 cm) long and weak ones about 1 inch (2.5 cm). Bear in mind that the harder you cut back, the stronger will be the subsequent growth in the following season. Floribundas are best left just a little longer.

Shrub roses are treated like deciduous shrubs (page 56): cut out a proportion of old wood each year but never more than a third of the bush.

Climbers and ramblers should also be cut back hard at planting time but thereafter the treatment differs slightly.

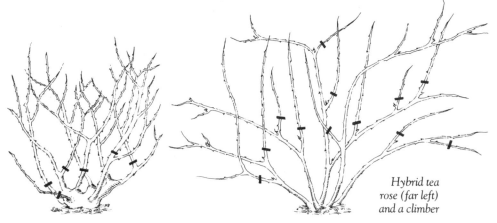

*Hybrid tea
rose (far left)
and a climber*

Climbers flower on the current season's growth and rarely produce shoots from the base. So it's best to train out a framework of shoots, tied into wires on the wall or fence. These will remain for some years, producing flowering growths along their length. They should be cut back to two or three buds each year in March. If this results, as it often does in certain varieties, in the production of strong, non-flowering growths, the best way to get them to flower well is to restrict the flow of sap by pulling them down horizontally and tying them in.

Ramblers have a different habit of growth and flowering. They flower for a single time each season and they do so on side shoots from wood made the previous year. After flowering, therefore, the shoots that have flowered should be cut right back to the ground while the younger, non-flowered wood is tied in in their place. If there aren't many of these new growths, you can retain a few of the older ones and prune back the side shoots to two buds.

*Leave one or two old
shoots if no young ones
are growing*

◆ *FRUIT TREES* ◆

Now, here's a real brain-teaser. Just read the instructions for pruning a fan-trained peach tree and, if you can understand them, perhaps you'd be good enough to explain them to me! I've never been able to grasp them. Yet, once again, if you know the *reasons* for pruning fruit, it really isn't difficult at all.

Apples and Pears

I'm convinced that new gardeners tend not to grow fruit mainly because the complicated pruning puts them off. I've therefore spent some time trying to devise simple ways to do it that are suitable for us amateurs. The answer is to grow small, trained trees which are, in any case, much more suitable for modern gardens.

Start by buying either one- or at most two-year-old trees, because they'll produce much earlier and also give you a chance to prune to the shape you want. The first thing is to learn how to prune a cordon and then the rest is easy.

A cordon is a single stem, which is usually planted at an angle of 45 degrees and trained on to either a fence or a post and wire structure.

If the plant you buy has any side shoots, cut them back to 3 inches (7.5 cm) long when you plant but leave the 'leading shoot' (the continuation of the main stem) unpruned. If there are no side shoots, there's no pruning to do until the following summer.

In August cut back all side shoots coming from the main stem to 3 inches (7.5 cm). In the first year that may well be all there is to do, but in the second there will also be extra shoots growing out of the side shoots. These should be cut back, again in August, to 1 inch (2.5 cm).

And that's all there is to it. Every August you cut shoots coming from the main stem to leave them 3 inches (7.5 cm) long and any sub-laterals coming from them to 1 inch (2.5 cm). That way you build up short, spiky 'spurs', and it's on those that you'll get the fruit.

If you want to be more adventurous, it's not difficult to grow a fan or an espalier. The difference is that, as well as pruning to produce fruiting spurs, you need to build the shape of the tree at the same time.

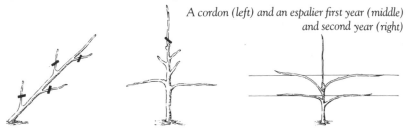

A cordon (left) and an espalier first year (middle) and second year (right)

An espalier has horizontal branches growing out from either side of the main stem at about 1 ft (30 cm) intervals. Again, it's trained on to wires. Once more you start with a one-year-old tree and, in the first winter, cut the leading shoot back to leave it just 1 inch (2.5 cm) or so higher than the first wire. During the first summer three or four branches will grow out. Two of them should be tied in to the wire, one on each side of the main stem, and a third should be trained to grow straight upwards.

In the second winter this upright shoot is cut back to 1 inch (2.5 cm) above the second wire and the process repeated to form the second tier of branches. You can carry on like this for two or three more years until the tree reaches the height you want.

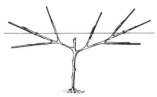

Then all you have to do to get fruiting spurs is to treat each branch exactly as if it were a cordon, pruning all shoots coming from the branch to 3 inches (7.5 cm) and any sub-laterals coming from them to 1 inch (2.5 cm).

A fan (*right*) is much the same. Again, start with a one-year-old tree, cut it back to about 1 ft (30 cm) above the ground and train the resulting shoots this time into a fan shape, tying them in to canes wired to the horizontal wires. Then treat each branch like a cordon.

Plums and Cherries

Grow plums and cherries as fans on a fence where you can control growth more easily and you can easily put on netting to protect the fruit from birds. You can generally buy trees already trained to the basic shape, but if not, train exactly as recommended for apples. The main difference with plums is that, because they are prone to silver leaf disease, the pruning is done in April when the tree will be growing strongly and the cuts will heal quickly.

All you have to do really with plums is to concentrate on covering the fence with shoots spaced about 3–4 inches (7.5–10 cm) apart. Start by removing any shoots that are growing straight out from the fence and any that are closer than 3–4 inches (7.5–10 cm). Tie in the shoots evenly and, when they start to outgrow their space, simply pinch out the growing tip.

After harvesting, cut back by about half any shoots you've pinched out previously.

Peaches

Fans are much the best way to grow peaches because you can then protect them against birds and peach-leaf curl. This fungus disease attacks almost unfailingly, leaving leaves red and blistered and reducing the vigour and fruitfulness of the tree. The spores are carried on rain; so if the plants can be protected with a temporary 'roof' slung from the fence, they'll escape attack and you won't need to cover them in pesticides. As for pruning – just read the instructions for fan peaches and your brain will be instantly addled. Yet an understanding of *why* you prune in that way makes it simple.

Divide it into two parts. The first few years are spent shaping the tree so that it covers the fence. Start by fixing wires about 1 ft (30 cm) apart on which to train the tree.

Plant a one-year-old tree and, in the first winter, cut it back to leave about 1½ ft (45 cm) from the ground. When it grows out, select two branches and tie these to canes fixed to the wires to form the base of the fan.

In subsequent years, select side shoots from these branches to fill any space available. The shoots should be about 4 inches (10 cm) apart, so, in the early spring, remove any shoots that are growing straight out from the wall and any that are closer together than 4 inches (10 cm). Tie the rest in to cover the fence evenly, and once they've grown as long as you want them, pinch out the growing tips. In the winter prune by about half those shoots you've pinched out.

From now on you start pruning for fruit. That's easy too, provided you realise that the fruit is borne on shoots that were made the previous season.

In mid- to late spring, look at the side shoots and, when they're about six leaves long and have made a replacement shoot at their base, pinch out the tip. That replacement will, of course, bear the fruit for the following year.

The fruit will be borne that year on the shoots you've pinched back to six leaves and these can be cut right out the following winter. The replacement shoot is tied in its place and the whole process starts again.

THE PERILS OF
◆ PLANT HUNTING ◆

by Roy Lancaster

In 1905 at a remote checkpoint in China's Yunnan province, the Scottish plant explorer George Forrest staggered into the arms of a welcoming official having survived one of the most relentless manhunts in plant-hunting history. For three weeks he had been pursued by armed bands of Tibetan monks with only revenge in mind. They had already tortured and put to death two of Forrest's companions – elderly French missionaries – together with a host of their Chinese converts, and the resourceful Scotsman, had it not been for his fitness and cunning, would have suffered a like fate.

Such was the resentment stirred up by 'interfering foreigners' during the early decades of the present century that life for a plant hunter in China was perilous indeed. But China was not the only challenge in the world of plant exploration. One of the unluckiest early plant explorers was the Czech Benedict Roezl who collected plants, especially orchids, in North, Central and South America during the second half of the last century. He was held up and robbed by bandits no less than seventeen times, while on another occasion he survived a confrontation with a disgruntled jaguar.

By comparison, today's plant explorers have an easy time of it and most of them face nothing more dangerous than falling rocks or a village dog. Having said that, there are few things more alarming than crossing a bamboo bridge when someone else is attempting to pass you in the opposite direction. This has happened to me more than once, but I shall never forget the first time in 1971 that I found myself on the 250 foot long bridge at Num in East Nepal.

Spanning a tributary of the River Arun, this remarkable structure, since replaced, trembled as soon as I set foot on it and swung and jumped in a disconcerting manner the further I progressed. I met my fellow traveller about mid-way where the bridge sagged. He was a native porter carrying a basket piled high with pots and pans. There appeared to be no way that we could safely pass, but without stopping to consider this fact he made to squeeze past me, his head bowed beneath the weight on his back. For several awful seconds the bridge lurched wildly while I clung to the side for dear life. Then my partner in this unlikely routine thrust ahead only to find his foot slipping through a gap in the bamboo matting floor. He made a desperate lunge for the rail which saved him but sent the entire contents of his basket in a noisy, silvery shower down into the river.

Cleaning seed in camp that night I wondered if those who had bought shares in our collections would ever fully appreciate how close their collector and their prize poppies and primulas had been to a watery grave!

It was in Nepal also that a vicious demon almost denied me and my colleagues the seed of a most beautiful dwarf rhododendron. We were on the final leg of a journey into a high alpine valley where it was rumoured many choice plants grew. The night before our arrival we camped in a dark forest – dark in the daytime, that is, because of the dense, leafy canopy above. In the dead of night we were awoken by a chilling scream and shortly afterwards – by now outside our tents – we were confronted by a very frightened porter who, according to our head sherpa, had been attending to his toilet when he was bitten by a demon. His shouts and antics had aroused his colleagues who, taking this to be a bad omen, were all for packing up and returning to the safety of the village in the valley below. We managed to calm them down, however, with a promise to search for and deal with the demon at first light.

It was a promise easily fulfilled, for when the porter led us to the site of the incident we found the assailant – a giant nettle – rising tall in a clearing and armed to the leaf! Later that day we entered the most beautiful valley and there found *Rhododendron ciliatum* forming extensive carpets and laden with seed.

A rarely advertised source of stress modern plant explorers occasionally encounter is the suicide driver. These are found in most countries but are especially dangerous in mountain areas of the world. He – it is always a male – turns what should be a quiet, uneventful journey into a nightmare remembered for the rest of one's life, always assuming, of course, that one survives. Some years ago I suffered such a journey across the Elburz Mountains of northern Iran. My companion (whom I shall call Albert), an employee of the then Ministry of Agriculture, Forests and Fisheries or some such title, was a remarkable fellow who combined the art of the contortionist with that of the driver. We were heading out on a weekend trip to see the forests above the Caspian shore and, it being winter, the wheels of our vehicle were securely bound with snow chains, though that did not prevent us sliding about on roads of intestinal complexity. Albert, who also doubled as cook, had come well prepared for our sojourn and the floor of his jeep was littered with bags and boxes, some of which were accommodated under his feet.

The journey was long and fraught and, perhaps in an effort to reduce the tension, Albert plied me with an endless supply of sweets and biscuits accompanied by a constant chatter in English that I had difficulty in understanding. To reach the sweetmeats entailed groping in sundry containers for which task – in order to free his hands – he guided the steering wheel with either his shoulders or his knees and once – in producing a delicacy from under his seat – with his head. The fact that this was my first visit to the Caspian encouraged Albert to point out local geography and places of interest along the way, which added further to my alarm, especially when, as always on a hazardous bend, we encountered a fully laden bus or truck careering apparently out of control. It did nothing for my peace of mind to note the legends sported by many of these vehicles trusting for their safe passage in the Will of Allah.

Suffice to say we managed to reach the Caspian shore in one piece and briefly explored those rich woodlands where Persian ironwood (*Parrotia persica*) and Cappadocian maple (*Acer cappadocicum*) dominated, their leaves aflame, their feet steeped in pools of pink and white cyclamen. Although the Caspian Forest, certainly for the foreseeable future, is inaccessible to Western travellers, there are many other wild areas of the world where plants can be observed in their natural state without the need for heroics or superhuman fitness. Several travel firms (see below for addresses) specialise in treks and tours to wilderness areas where, often under expert guidance, plants familiar from gardens can be studied and photographed where *they* choose to grow rather than where gardeners put them. I mention photography because this has become the most satisfying and sensible method of recording one's finds rather than digging them up for a risky passage back home and an uncertain future in cultivation. Wild seed collecting is best left to the scientists and conservationists.

Travels in China; A Plantsman's Paradise by Roy Lancaster (Summerfield Books, Cumbria)

TRAVEL COMPANIES OFFERING BOTANICAL ♦ HOLIDAYS ♦

Garden Tours,
Premier Suite,
Central Business Exchange,
Central Milton Keynes,
Buckinghamshire.
(Tel. 0908 609551)
Italy, France, Portugal

Gardeners Delight Holidays,
J.A.R. Services,
Garden House,
45 Church Road,
Saxilby,
Lincoln LN1 2HH.
(Tel. 0522 703773)
Britain and overseas

Nature Trek,
40 The Dean,
Alresford,
Hampshire SO24 9AZ.
(Tel. 0962 733051)
Nepal, Kashmir, Kenya, Zambia, Botswana, Ethiopia, Australia, Galapagos, New Zealand, Indonesia

Prospect Garden Tours,
10 Barley Mow Passage,
London W4 4PH.
(Tel. 01-995 2151)
British gardens

Raoul Moxley Travel,
76 Elmbourne Road,
London SW17 8JJ.
(Tel. 01-672 2437)
New list of destinations available for 1990

Voyages Jules Verne,
21 Dorset Square,
London NW1 6QG.
(Tel. 01-724 6624)
Spain, Greece, France, Italy, Switzerland, Austria, Cyprus, Canada, Mallorca, Turkey, Russia

LEARNING THE
◆ HARD WAY ◆

by Phil Franklin

Most of gardening is only the sum of other people's experience; the problem is, which people do you listen to? Are their soil and weather conditions the same as your own? Do they use magic potions?

I realise now that the only way of finding out is to try what they recommend, and if it does not work then try something else the following year. If only I had stuck to this principle two years ago, when I swapped my small suburban garden for my present acre and a half of land and overcome my innate impatience and the strong belief that I knew better than the experts, I could have saved myself from unnecessary problems. There will be those who will no doubt scoff and then go on to make the same mistakes as me. I hope that those who are more humble may learn just a little from my errors.

The paddock which ran alongside the existing garden of my new house was just crying out to be the garden of my dreams. To be faced with virgin pasture like this was like having a new exercise book and looking forward to filling in the first page in your best handwriting, yet knowing that the rest would be scribble as you did your best to catch up with the class. The sober and sensible side of my nature acknowledged that it was going to be six or seven years before it even started to look like a garden. Turning over the soil for the first time, I think, released a small garden devil that perched on my shoulder and told me that I could have a fully mature garden by the following spring. I should have ignored him.

It was November when we moved in after a wonderful autumn and that posed the first problem. What to do first? Draw plans? Remove hedges and plant new ones or start digging? In the event, I gave it fully three minutes thought before charging in like a demented bull and did everything at once.

Part of the hedge that divided the existing garden from the paddock needed to come out, so a kindly neighbour came along, complete with tractor and chains, and hauled it out. Had I dosed the hedgerow with weedkiller first, I would not now still be enjoying the annual display of goosegrass, creeping buttercup, docks and thistles in that part of the garden. I did think ahead with the paddock, though. I sprayed it with quantities of glyphosate to rid it permanently of perennial weeds: a wise and clever thing to do, if it is applied at the right time – but November is not the right time.

In my haste to start digging I quite forgot that for a hormone weedkiller to work properly, the plants need to be growing strongly so that the entire plant can become fully impregnated. The top growth died back well enough and soon showed how successful my bright idea of marking out the future shape of the garden in weedkiller was. The neat rectangles of the vegetable garden and the curves of the flower beds were graphically illustrated by seemingly dying and brown weeds.

It was only the following spring that it dawned on me that, by digging too early, I had neatly sliced up some of the weeds into thousands of rooted cuttings. It did prove the experts right when they say that a rooted cutting has a vigour far outstripping that of the parent plant.

From this experience I learned (the hard way) Lesson One: read what it says on the bottle three times, and then do as it says. Better still, if you have a sizeable area of weeds to clear, hack and trample them down as best you can, spread thick, opaque polythene over the area, weight it down with soil round the edges and leave it for a full growing season. I have tried this method too and it's far better than using a chemical weedkiller, for not only do you get rid of the weeds, but by the time you remove the polythene, the worms have already mixed the dead and composted weeds into the soil.

I am extremely lucky in having wonderful soil, a medium loam that has probably been undisturbed meadowland for centuries – but I nearly destroyed it overnight in my haste to get in my first crop. Next door to my house is a livery stable with vast quantities of horse manure sitting in a field unwanted and unloved. Barrow-loads of this precious material was dug into the soil; however, I little realised at the time that it was principally wood shavings. The effect of all this unrotted material was to denude my soil of nearly all its nitrogen, the soil bacteria consuming copious amounts of it to break the wood shavings down. Two years and pounds' worth of bought-in artificial nitrogen later, the soil is back in good heart and growing me plenty of good-quality vegetables. The silly thing is, I could have waited a year before putting anything into the soil: because of its uncultivated state, nature had already balanced its needs.

Having a plentiful supply of manure has, in a curious way, saved me some labour. It is always said in gardening circles that growing potatoes will help clear the ground and in a way it does, but this is due only to the hard work you put into digging, planting and earthing up, and it is this latter task that I find particularly irksome. Instead of earthing up the potatoes for a second time, I apply a thick mulch of manure. It is easier, the mulch helps suppress weeds and it conserves moisture during the long, dry days of summer.

Working to a tight budget in a garden is an eminently sensible thing to do; meanness, on the other hand, can be counter-productive. I learnt this lesson when it came to sowing a new lawn. Working on the principle that a single grass seed can produce a plant 3 inches (7.5 cm) in diameter, I deduced that the seed merchants' rate of application was not only profligate but also a confidence trick, designed to part me from my hard-earned cash. It was obvious, therefore, that one could halve the recommended number of ounces of seed per square yard and still have a lawn the envy of the neighbourhood.

Three months later this elegant theory was in tatters. The grass grew well enough, but so did the weeds which, on hearing of the vast, uncultivated areas between the grass plants, came in droves to set up home. The perfect microclimate between the sparse tufts of grass was ideal for the propagation of buttercups, dandelions and plantain. Dear seed merchants, I am sorry to have doubted you.

I am lucky enough to have plenty of space, indeed space enough to grow such quantities of my favourite vegetable, runner beans, that I can eat them every day and still have some left for freezing. The first year they grew well and the flower buds were starting to blush crimson when I noticed clusters of blackfly on the tips. Panic sent me to the shed to get out the sprayer and drown them with insecticide. The blackfly died. So did the beans. I had not washed out the sprayer after using weedkiller and, even at this weak dilution, the residue was enough to destroy that season's crop.

There are two morals to this sorry tale:

1 If you must spray, have one sprayer marked 'insecticide' and one marked 'weedkiller'.

2 Better still, don't use insecticides at all.

I have been taking this second course of action more recently and I am now leaving the job of aphid clearance to ladybirds, hoverflies and blue tits. Last year my plants were not too badly affected, but perhaps I was lucky.

A little knowledge need not always be a dangerous thing. I know two facts: moles eat worms and they have to eat lots of them just to stay alive, let alone make merry. When I spied a line of molehills in a neighbouring field starting to head for my newly sown lawn, this insight into a mole's metabolism proved useful. Working on the principle of 'no worms, no moles', I watered in an 8 ft (2.4 m) mole break of wormkiller along the edge of the lawn – not something one does lightly, but it worked. The line of molehills ricocheted off the worm-free area at a 45 degree angle and back across the field. The worms were back at full strength six months later and the moles lived to tunnel another day.

Alas, having bright ideas is often the result of an untidy mind. This and the misguided belief that I will always remember what I have planted where, without the aid of labels, has landed me in trouble on more than one occasion. Two years ago I planted an early potato, whose name I was sure to remember. It turned out to be a rotten cooker, breaking up in the water seconds after it came to the boil. Had I remembered the name, I could have avoided buying exactly the same variety the following year and making the same mistake again. I still don't know the name.

It's the same with bulbs and other plants that die back in winter. They all become victim to my spade, getting spliced, spiked or mashed, all for the want of a label.

After two years I am now starting to calm down and work at nature's pace. No more planting out bedding plants too early and having them killed by a late frost. No more working in the garden when it's too wet. I am learning that there is plenty of time for everything, except weeding. I have started to spend time looking at what I have now and not waiting anxiously for what I may have in the future. We seem to spend so little time just appreciating the brilliant blue of a forget-me-not or the extraordinary geometry of an unfolding fern.

I am quite pleased with what I have achieved so far: 300 square yards of productive vegetable plot, lawns that are now starting to look good and, through friends and visiting good nurseries, a number of interesting plants. I am not sure that this is quite good enough for a visit from *Gardeners' World* yet, apart from which I still don't think I can remember what I have planted where.

The experts may not be right all of the time, but they are right more times than not. From now on I shall listen to their advice and act on it.

HOUSEPLANTS: FROM BABIES TO
◆ GRANNIES ◆

by Anne Swithinbank

Some houseplant owners acquire plants for purely aesthetic reasons. To them plants are ornaments and are chosen because they are the right size, shape and colour for a particular corner. If they look pretty by the radiator, they are left there to frizzle up and are thrown out when no longer attractive.

This point of view would be anathema to the second category of houseplant owners who enjoy the challenge of keeping an interesting collection of plants alive and well for as long as possible. These are the people who choose their plants very carefully, often exchanging cuttings of unusual plants rather than buying them fully grown. Great care is taken to give the plant everything it needs by way of correct position for light, temperature and humidity, enough but not too much water and feed. Under these circumstances some plants will last for many years. I still have a bird's nest fern (*Asplenium nidus*) which left home with me when I began my horticultural training at Kew Gardens. This plant must be at least fifteen years old and has survived six house moves over the years.

Between these two types of grower there are those who no longer have a casual throw-away attitude to their plants but have not yet acquired the expertise to grow them really well or know what to expect of them. It is to be hoped that this section of the book will help them understand more about plants and set them on the road to becoming real enthusiasts.

◆ STARTING A COLLECTION ◆

Buying Plants

A trip to the garden centre or florist can be a confusing experience for those whose houseplant education is at the infant stage. My advice to a complete novice would be to start with commonly grown plants that are able to withstand some low light and some fluctuation in temperature, are not normally attacked by pests and tend to carry on looking good for a long time without extra attention. These are usually affordable and can be used as 'guinea pigs' before you splash out on more exotic specimens.

Houseplants that are easy to grow include the rosary plant (*Ceropegia woodii*), a trailing but very easy succulent; the small parlour palm (*Chamaedorea elegans*); *Dracaena deremensis* 'White Stripe', a striking, medium-sized, foliage plant; the rubber plant (*Ficus elastica*); a variegated form of the creeping fig (*Ficus pumila* 'Sunny') which has small leaves and will trail over the edge of a pot; grape ivy (*Rhoicissus rhomboidea*), a tough but attractive climber; devil's ivy (*Scindapsus aureus*), a most attractive variegated climber or trailer; peace lily (*Spathiphyllum*), attractive as a foliage plant but bearing white, arum lily-type flowers; cape primrose (*Streptocarpus*), an easy plant to keep in flower provided the temperature stays warm and care is taken not to splash water on its leaves; and the piggy back plant (*Tolmiea menziesii*), whose soft, hairy leaves sprout new plants where leaf joins stem.

Examine your chosen plant carefully. You are looking for a compact plant sitting securely in its pot with healthy shoots and no damaged leaves. Avoid anything which rocks about it the pot. Check to make sure there are no pests. Many pests like greenfly, mealy bug and scale insect secrete a sugary honeydew which falls on to the leaves below. Sooty mould begins to feed and grow on the honeydew and makes an unsightly mask of black over the leaf. The most difficult pest to spot is spider mite. In this case leaves take on a dry, speckled look and eventually become scorched and papery. The mites are very small and pale brownish yellow in colour with two dots. Heavy infestations culminate with webbing around leaves and shoots but you are most unlikely to find anything as obvious as this at a garden centre.

Unless you are buying seasonal plants in flower, winter is generally a bad time to buy plants. Always be suspicious, at this time of year, of plants displayed outside. They may have suffered damage from frost or cold wind which will not begin to show until you get them home. Insist that any indoor plant bought during cold weather is well wrapped as even a brief exposure to frost on the journey home is enough to kill some of them. The worst problem is trying to acclimatise new plants to the conditions of low light, dry air and fluctuating temperatures often found indoors during winter which causes some plants to drop flower buds, others to develop scorch marks on their leaves and yet more to wither and die completely. The same plants bought in summer would be able to adjust slowly to any adverse conditions and are less likely to die from shock as a result. Just think of how these plants would have been cosseted in their glasshouse nurseries before being sold.

Sowing Seed

A cheap but fascinating way to raise your own houseplants is by seed. There is a good range of houseplant seed of various kinds to be found in the seed catalogues. Send off for the catalogues before Christmas so that you can spend the Christmas holidays browsing through. Although seed should arrive in early spring, unless specified otherwise I would delay sowing until May when more light and even temperatures are available for germination and growing on.

All you need by way of equipment is a few small, clean pots – ones measuring 3½ inches (9 cm) across the top are ideal – and some multi-purpose peat-based compost which will serve for sowing, pricking out and potting up. The method for all seed is to fill the pot loosely and firm down the surface. Stand the prepared pots on a firm surface outside and water using a can fitted with a rose so as not to disturb the compost. Allow the water to soak in before sowing. Large seed can be spaced out on the surface and pushed in so that it becomes buried by its own size with compost. Smaller seed should either be surface sown or very slightly covered with a fine scattering of compost. In both cases press the surface gently so that the seed is really nestled in amongst the moist, peaty particles. The seed packet should carry instructions about whether or not to cover with compost.

Large seed (left) and small seed (middle) can be germinated in the airing cupboard sealed under a plastic bag (right)

Most houseplant seed can be germinated in the airing cupboard. Cover the pot with cling-film or place inside a plastic bag and seal it. Place the pot on a shelf away from the tank otherwise it might be too warm for the seeds. The most important point is to look at the pot every day. As soon as germination begins, the pot must be moved to a windowsill (usually not south-facing as this is too bright) or a good light position. If you leave the seedlings in the cupboard, they will become long, drawn and no good. Seed like those of bird of paradise plant (*Strelitzia*), coffee (*Coffea arabica*), *Citrus* species and banana (*Musa*) can be germinated this way.

Seed which must have light to germinate and might find the airing cupboard too warm should be germinated in good but not direct light. Again, cover the pot with clear plastic. This treatment applies to indoor figs including the rubber plant (*Ficus* species), living stones (*Lithops*) and the sensitive plant (*Mimosa pudica*). Other good plants easily raised from seed on a windowsill include asparagus, umbrella plants (try *Cyperus diffusus*, which is more compact and shorter than the usual *C. alternifolius*), castor-oil plant (*Fatsia japonica*), *Philodendron* and West Indian holly (*Leea coccinea*), an attractive foliage plant.

Some of the larger, harder seed are better soaked for 24 hours prior to sowing in water which should start off lukewarm. Should germination take place but the seedling appear to stop growing, the best thing to do is prick it out to another pot, even if very small. Sometimes a root is produced, but no shoot. Again, transfer singly to longer pots and shoots will grow. Should fine seed, surface-sown, fail to germinate, try covering the next batch (never give up!) with fine vermiculite which allows light through but gives the seed some protection.

When seed has germinated, take off the plastic covering. When the seedlings are large enough, prick out either one to a pot or, if the seedlings are tiny, several to a pot but so that they have room to grow on. Always handle seedlings by their leaves so as not to bruise their stems (*right*).

A Trip to the Greengrocer's

Exotic fruit are fun to choose and eat but are also interesting to grow from pips, stones and stems. Unfortunately, it is most unlikely that any of them will bear fruit indoors, but they are worth growing for their foliage. You can germinate most of them in the airing cupboard.

Lychee (Litchi chinensis) has been cultivated in China for over two thousand years for its popular fruit. Probably a native of tropical Malaya, it makes a small tree when grown outside in warmer countries. As a houseplant it is worth having for its dainty, evergreen leaves which are a delightful shrimp pink when new. The seed is large and beautiful. Sow as soon as it comes from the fruit as it will not keep. My latest batch were sown in February and germinated within two weeks of being placed in the airing cupboard. The resulting plants were slow to grow at first, but after 3 months are now 6 inches (15 cm) high in 4 inch (10 cm) pots. They like to be kept moist and, although they are said to be lime haters, seem to be thriving with regular doses of fairly hard water.

Mango (Mangifera indica) is another tree of Malaysian and East Indian origin. The fruit is now widely available, though expensive, and if you can grow an interesting, large houseplant as well as enjoying the fruit, you will have had your money's worth. The seed is large and covered with fibrous strands of fruit. These should be scraped off before sowing otherwise the whole thing tends to rot away. Sow upright in a 4 inch (10 cm) pot with the pointed end of the seed just below the surface. Again, place the pot in the airing cupboard and after 2–3 weeks a thick shoot will appear. Leave for a few days until the shoot is a little bigger before bringing into a warm, light place to grow on. Be warned that these will make large houseplants.

Date palm (Phoenix dactylifera) is not always successful from seed: the stones that come out of the dates are not always fertile. However, it is worth persevering with them either in a warm room or the airing cupboard. The resulting small palms are very slow-growing, and the warmer the room they are given, the better.

Passion fruit (Passiflora edulis), a native of tropical South America, is very easy to germinate. Usually, once the fruit has been opened, the seeds are eaten along with the juicy pulp. However, save a few and sow them just under the surface of some compost. A windowsill will be adequate for germination. Seedlings must have really good light to develop well and if they do, a fine climbing plant will result. Flowers should be formed about 3 years from sowing. I have never tried to fruit them indoors but this is certainly possible in a conservatory.

Pineapple (Ananas comosus) is propagated not by seed but by cutting the tuft of leaves away from the fruit and encouraging it to grow roots from the stem. When removing the leaves, cut away about ½ inch (1 cm) of flesh with them. Trim the fleshy part off and remove some of the smaller bottom leaves (*below left*). Stand the exposed stem in water (*middle*) until short, tough little roots appear. This may take a month or more so be prepared to change the water and continue to clean the stem by removing any rotting leaves. After the roots have appeared, the plant can be potted into a peat-based compost with a little added sharp sand. The result will be a handsome foliage plant (*right*).

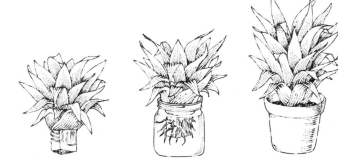

Cuttings

One of the best ways of succeeding with houseplants is to visit the homes of experienced growers. Look around to see which plants they have chosen for problem areas such as corners with little light, draughty passageways or near a radiator, and ask if they can spare a cutting. You will also ensure, this way, that you are getting a plant potentially as good as theirs because your cutting should grow up to resemble its parent in all ways.

Take the cutting, leaf or plantlet home in a sealed plastic bag to prevent undue wilting and deal with it as soon as possible. An amazing number of mostly soft-stemmed houseplant cuttings will root well in water, but all should root in a small pot containing a mixture of equal parts of sharp sand and peat, or equal amounts of vermiculite and peat. For conventional cuttings, cut under a node (the area on the stem where the leaves arise), strip off the bottom leaves, dip into fresh hormone rooting powder and dibble into cutting compost. Water in, place the whole pot inside a plastic bag and knot loosely to close. Keep warm and light but away from direct sun. Pitfalls include making the cutting too long – 3 inches (7.5 cm) is a good average – and setting only one cutting per pot. Crowd in as many (of one type) as possible and they will root better.

◆ HOW LONG WILL YOUR PLANTS LIVE? ◆

Temporary Plants

Annuals are plants which germinate from seed, grow, flower, produce more seed and die all in one season. Some of our houseplants belong in this category and really should be viewed only as a long-term bunch of flowers. Others, although not strictly annual, become so straggly and unlikely to flower again that they are best treated as such. Cineraria, browallia, calceolaria, pot chrysanthemums, *Exacum affine*, eustoma (*Lisianthus*) and *Primula malacoides* belong in this group. *Kalanchoe blossfeldiana* hybrids can be pruned after flowering and coaxed back into flower. Winter cherry (*Solanum capsicastrum*) can be pruned hard, placed outside for the summer and brought back in for a fresh show of winter berries. Poinsettia (*Euphorbia pulcherrima*) can also be allowed to go dormant after flowering, pruned, watered and encouraged to grow bracts. *Primula obconica* should carry on flowering for 2–3 years before giving up. However, none of these is ever as good as it was first time around.

Other temporary plants can be grown on from year to year but either go dormant or need a break from the house during the summer.

Hot water plant (Achimenes) is in the same family as African violets and hates water on its leaves. By the end of summer it will have died down and should be dried off and left all winter in a warm place. March is a good month for turning the compost out of the pot and searching for the maggot-like tubercles. Fill a shallow seedtray with peat-based compost and plant the tubercles in this. When they begin to grow, transfer them about six to a 5 inch (12.5 cm) pot. Take care not to overwater the plants and they will flower exotically given good (but not direct) light.

Cyclamen are well worth growing from year to year. At the time of writing I have just enjoyed my plant, in its second year, flowering all winter. After a long flowering period the plant will show no further signs of buds or leaves coming from the corm. This is a signal to cease watering and allow the plant to go dormant (usually in mid-April). I leave mine on its west-facing windowsill to feel the sun on the corm much as the original *Cyclamen persicum* might under its native Mediterranean sun. After a few weeks of this I place the pot somewhere cool and dry. Around September signs of growth appear which are the signal to start watering again. As new leaves appear the plant can be re-potted, but this is necessary only every 3–4 years and is really just a case of replacing old compost with new. Remember that these plants must have cool, light conditions in winter (mine loves a west-facing bedroom windowsill) otherwise they will turn yellow and collapse.

Gloxinia (Sinningia) is grown from a tuber which should be started off in a shallow tray of moist peat in February or March. Related to achimenes, it also dislikes water splashes on its leaves. After flowering, as the leaves turn yellow, stop watering and keep the tuber warm and dry over winter until taking it out of its pot to be started off again.

Azalea (Rhododendron simsii hybrids) is often in a pretty poor state by the time it has finished flowering and put up with low light and hot, dry air all winter. It likes to be moist at the roots all the time (never allow it to dry out), humid, cool and light, a combination which is very difficult to achieve in most houses. However, as soon as all danger of frost is past it can be placed outside in a position of dappled shade, plunged into the soil if it is acid or into a bucket of peat if not. A feed of iron sequestrine and regular watering throughout the summer will work wonders and a much-rejuvenated plant will be ready to go back indoors before the first frosts in autumn. Remember that azaleas dislike hard water.

Cymbidium orchids are often difficult to persuade into flower again. The secret is to treat them much like an azalea by giving them a summer break in the garden in dappled shade. Remember also to feed them regularly with a well-balanced high-potash feed (Chempak is very good) which will encourage flowering. Early-flowering varieties might even have flower spikes appearing by the time they are taken back into the house in September. They will then need good light to flower well. Plants flower better when pot-bound, so re-pot only when absolutely necessary and use a special orchid compost. The time to do this would be after flowering.

Hydrangea macrophylla hybrids are often sold as houseplants. Keep them cool, light and airy in the house and they will last for a long time. After flowering and when all danger of frost is past, they can be planted out in the garden. They will then be completely hardy and can remain outside. Remember that blue flowers will tend to turn pink on an alkaline soil, and pink ones blue on an acid soil. Add peat or lime to help correct this.

Permanent Houseplants

Permanent houseplants are those that, once settled in and growing well, could reasonably be expected to last for some years. Many of these plants have their origin in what we could call the wet tropics of the world: the forests of high temperature and high rainfall. The reason why so many plants from these regions make good houseplants is that they naturally grow in shady places. Some, for example spathiphyllum and dieffenbachia (this one is poisonous), would grow on the forest floor; others, like Swiss cheese plant *(Monstera)* and philodendron would climb up the trunks of trees, sending out aerial roots with which to cling and to send back down to the ground as extra support. Many of our popular houseplants would not naturally grow in soil as we might suppose but live epiphytically, clinging to the branches of trees or nestling in small niches high up in the tree trunks. These plants, including most orchids, many ferns, some begonias, flamingo flowers *(Anthurium)*, and most of the urn plants and air plants (bromeliads) are not parasites but use their hosts merely for anchorage. They are able to absorb all the moisture and nourishment they require through their leaves and roots. The saturated atmosphere of the forest and rapid rate of decay give them a ready source of water and nutrients.

If you can imagine the natural habitat that might be enjoyed by such plants, you can appreciate how they require an even, warm temperature and good humidity. The epiphytes grown indoors in pots, in particular, are susceptible to overwatering as their roots are used to plenty of air.

The more shrubby, tropical, temperate and Mediterranean plants such as shrimp plant *(Beloperone guttata)*, lollipop plant *(Pachystachys lutea)*, yesterday, today and tomorrow plant *(Brunfelsia calycina* 'Macrantha'), hibiscus and pelargonium, which we grow mostly for their flowers, require more work to keep them looking good. These tend to become straggly very quickly and need to be either pruned or propagated regularly to keep them in shape. Nevertheless, having acquired the stock, it should be possible to keep them going indefinitely. This also applies to trailing plants like goldfish or lipstick plant *(Columnea)* and wandering Jew *(Tradescantia)*. When these plants become old and tired, take cuttings from the tips and grow them on as replacements. Meanwhile, prune the original plant hard, cutting back newer shoots to within one or two nodes of older stems. Place in the light and they should grow again.

WHAT MAKES
◆ A PLANT? ◆

by Stefan Buczacki

I always think it a great shame that schoolchildren relish most the animal parts of their biology lessons and find plants relatively boring. Admittedly, most animals can run around and display at least a degree of personality, but biologically a plant is a much more exciting object. For animals depend directly or indirectly on plants for their very existence – herbivores eat them and carnivores eat herbivores. By contrast, plants are more or less self-sufficient: put a plant into some soil and it will not only conjure up food materials as if by magic from nowhere and thus grow and thrive, but it will produce offspring and perpetuate its species too. How does it manage this? From whence comes the wherewithal for this independent-minded and very sophisticated way of life?

A plant, in common with any other living thing (you and I included) is really no more or less than a bag of chemicals. So let's consider first the way in which this bag is constructed and some of the chemicals that it contains. You will need an imaginary microscope to appreciate the construction, for the bag is composed of many thousands of smaller bags called cells. Cells vary in size depending on their particular role within the plant but are infrequently larger than about one fifty-thousandth of a millimetre – hence the need for the microscope. They each contain a controlling body, the nucleus, with other essential minute structures floating in a watery liquid called protoplasm. Groups of cells of similar type and function are massed together to form tissues, and it is the groups of tissues that together make up the whole plant as we see it.

From what I have said about the watery liquid contained in all cells, you will now understand why I think of water as the key ingredient of plants and why I consider careful attention to watering as the most important single operation that any gardener ever does. This is an importance that will be even more apparent when I explain some of the key roles that water plays in plant life.

However, having come to regard a plant as a bag of watery chemicals, you may

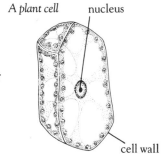

A plant cell   nucleus

cell wall

understandably wonder how the whole thing stays upright. And how, in the case of the truly huge pieces of vegetation called forest trees, such a massive object can ever be founded on something as apparently feeble. In fact water is not as feeble as you might think – imagine a flimsy piece of rubber such as a deflated balloon and then fill this with water. Certainly you must handle it carefully to prevent it from bursting, but it is perfectly possible for such a 'watery bag' to support a fairly considerable weight. Multiply the balloon many thousands of times and you really do have something pretty substantial. Seedlings and small plants rely more or less on this system alone, but to support a large and permanent above-ground framework, such as that of a shrub or tree, there is an additional structure involved too; one that can perhaps be compared with an outside skeleton. For the watery bags or balloons are encased in a more rigid framework called a cell wall. (And it is the possession of this rigid wall that sets plant cells apart from animal cells. They depend on a different supporting device, an overall skeleton tissue made up from very specialised cells; not internal, as in humans and other large creatures, but external as in the case of such lower beings as insects and lobsters.) The plant cell wall always contains a rather tough chemical allied to sugar. It is called cellulose – you will be familiar with its toughness in cellophane paper. But even this is insufficient on its own to support a tree. There the cell walls contain another, highly complex chemical called lignin; and tissues containing lignified cells are called wood.

The fact that plant cells have a rigid wall around them helps explain the first of the two questions that my balloon analogy must raise. For this wall does much to prevent the balloon from bursting. After all, you can handle most plants fairly roughly without their falling apart and depositing a puddle on the floor, although you must be especially careful with seedlings which have only a very thin layer of cellulose to help them, and certainly no lignin. But the second question is even more puzzling – how does the water find its way into the 'balloon' and then stay there without leaking out again? And this is a plot that thickens further when I tell you that the cell wall and the balloon inside it (let's now give it its proper name of cell membrane) are actually permeable to water – it can pass right through. The answer lies with an extraordinary process called osmosis. It is a simple matter of physical chemistry that if there is water or a weak solution on one side of such a membrane and a stronger solution of chemical salts on the other, the water will pass from the weaker to the stronger – in effect, in an attempt to dilute the stronger and equate the two solutions. I have already said that the cell contains chemicals, and these therefore serve to draw in water from the outside – and, once they have entered, the internal solution exerts a pressure on the membrane, just like that in a water-filled balloon, to hold it rigidly.

The cells into which water from the soil first passes are the fragile root hairs – those cottonwool-like growths that you see when a seed germinates and first puts out a young rootlet. For the water to pass from there into the stem and leaves, other processes are involved of which the most important depends on evaporation. At the other end of the plant, on the leaves, are tiny pores called stomata. The drying effect of the sun and wind draws water from these pores and so pulls up more minute capillary tubes (themselves, of course, formed from specialised cells) to replace it. So the entire plant is held firmly upright and is well furnished with water.

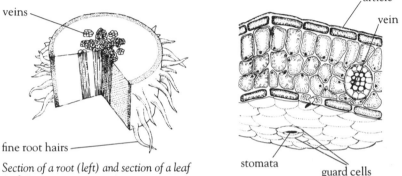

Section of a root (left) and section of a leaf (right)

However, the water that passes in from the soil has another function. Although weaker than the solution in the cells, it nonetheless contains mineral substances dissolved from the soil. As it passes into the root cells, it takes these mineral substances with it and so the plant obtains its supply of basic nutritional elements. And the N (nitrogen), P (phosphate), K (potash), and other mineral elements that we apply as fertiliser, dissolve in the soil into their basic constituents and so enter the plant in the same manner. So we now have one explanation of the way that the 'magic' nutrients are obtained to enable plants to thrive independently of other plants, animals or other outside forces. My reference to fertiliser actually suggests that garden plants depend on us, but actually this is not the case. We use it because we want them to perform rather more dramatically than their wild relatives. Without fertiliser, we would still have cabbages and dahlias; they would simply be rather like wild cabbages and wild dahlias and unlikely to win prizes or make us feel particularly effective gardeners.

Mineral nutrients obtained from the soil through root hairs supply only part of a plant's food needs. And it is in its way of obtaining the remainder that plant life seems closest to magic and is a primary reason why I think that plants are such extraordinarily wonderful objects. For they manufacture the remainder of their food from thin air. In fact, the air is not as thin as we all tend to assume: it contains a blend of several different gases. The bulk is made up of nitrogen and oxygen but it is two of the smaller components that interest us here – carbon dioxide which comprises about 0.03 per cent and that splendid material water again which, as water vapour, ranges up to about 4 per cent. (In passing, perhaps it is worth mentioning that although nitrogen from the air is of no use to plants directly, some of it does find its way into members of the pea and bean family when the bacteria that live in the nodules present on their roots 'fix' or convert it into a form that, after further chemical changes, becomes part of the soil nitrate pool.)

The equation by which plants use atmospheric gases to manufacture food says: carbon dioxide plus water (plus some energy – see below for where this comes from) equals carbohydrate plus oxygen. Carbohydrates are the key to the matter for they cover a large range of chemicals (sugars and starch are familiar examples but cellulose, which I have already mentioned, is another) that have two quite distinct roles. The first is that they can be used directly or indirectly as building materials to manufacture new cells and enhance growth. But the second is more subtle for they also act as carriers of energy and can be used to release this later. The energy taken in to power the chemical equation given above is released when the equation is reversed – oxygen plus carbohydrate equals carbon dioxide plus water (and energy). Moreover, carbohydrates can be stored within the tissues to be used in this way at some future date. When we harvest and eat plant products, we are tapping in to this energy reserve and using it for our own purposes.

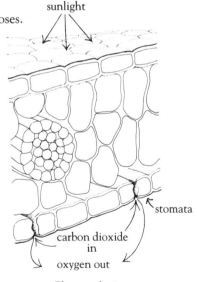

The two more or less opposite processes that I have outlined have distinct and familiar names. The energy release using oxygen is called respiration. But the energy capture and carbohydrate manufacture is the really fascinating process. It is called photosynthesis and it is unique to green plants, the key lying in the fact that they *are* green. For the green colour in plants is imparted by a substance called chlorophyll. This is the substance that traps the energy contained in sunlight and uses it to power the reaction in which carbohydrate is manufactured. Chlorophyll isn't present in all plant cells – there would be little point in it occurring in cells deep within the body of the plant where sunlight

sunlight

stomata

carbon dioxide in

oxygen out

Photosynthesis

cannot reach. But in almost all cells at the surface and above ground, chlorophyll is there, reaching its greatest concentration in the leaves.

The leaf is one of the classic examples of the relationship between form and function. It is constructed in such a way that it exposes the maximum number of chlorophyll-containing cells to the sunlight and yet also has to effect a compromise with its water regulatory roles. Some water must be allowed to evaporate through the pores to bring about the flow up the plant described earlier. But there must not be too much evaporation or the plant will begin to lose water faster than its roots can replace it. Then, some will be drawn out from the cell 'balloons', structural rigidity will diminish and wilting and perhaps irreparable damage will ensue. It may have occurred to you that some of your garden plants have not green, but red, purple or mottled leaves. Nonetheless, you need have no fear that they can't photosynthesise: the chlorophyll is there but it is simply masked to our eyes by other stronger-coloured pigments.

So far, I have described plants as individuals. However, nature is a selfless mistress and the sole role of the individual plant is to ensure that its species as a whole continues. It may sound simplistic, but the essential purpose of all living things – animals as well as plants – is to reproduce themselves. Plants do this in two main ways, one comparable with the reproduction with which we are familiar in more advanced animals and the other that has a counterpart only in the most primitive members of the animal kingdom. The method that plants share with the likes of amoebae and some lowly worms is what in gardening is called vegetative reproduction. This is a process that involves some part of one individual detaching itself and thence growing independently to form a new plant. The part can take several forms – specially modified stems, such as rhizomes, runners, offsets or stolons, or modified roots such as those that give rise to suckers are familiar examples, although the production of bulbs, bulbils, corms

A rhizome (left) and a bulb (right)

and some tubers are all other instances. As the new offspring are formed from part of their parent's tissues, they are identical genetically and will therefore perpetuate any attributes, good or bad, that the parent possesses.

But the principal method of plant reproduction, as in higher animals, is through the medium of sex – specially modified cells from one sex, the male, are transferred to enable them to fuse with comparable cells on the female. The advantage of sexual reproduction of course is that it allows transfer and exchange of genetic information or genes. So the offspring contain a blend of the genes of their parents and hence combine attributes of both. In plants the structures that contain the sex cells are flowers, and in many cases it is difficult superficially to distinguish the male from the female. Close examination will reveal, however, whether male stamens containing pollen or female stigmas attached to ovaries are present, but the situation is complicated by the fact that different plant species vary in the disposition of the sexual organs. Some flowers contain both male and female structures, some contain only one, but may bear both sexes either on the same plant or separately. Moreover, there are degrees to which male cells from one plant, be they from the same or separate flowers, can fertilise female cells from the same individual.

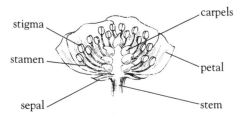

Evolutionarily, a flower is a telescoped leafy shoot in which the shoot tip has become altered to form stigma and ovary and the leaves have lost their green chlorophyll, developed other pigments and become more fragile – we call them petals. And then some of the petals have become modified still further to form stamens. The modifications take many and varied forms and we should be grateful that they do, for this gives rise to the astonishing range and beauty of the flowers that we cultivate. However, all are essentially devices to ensure that efficient pollen transfer takes place. The bright colours and ability to produce nectar are designed not to attract you and me, but insects or other creatures that will carry the pollen. And only in this respect are plants at all dependent on animals for their well-being. Moreover, as if to prove that even this is an unimportant embellishment, many flowers rely not on insects at all but on the wind to blow pollen from one to the other – catkins and the entire grass family are common examples of this botanical independence. They are, after all, and as I stated at the beginning of this chapter, very exciting objects.

COURSES ON
◆ GARDENING ◆

For those wishing to extend their knowledge of gardening, both theoretical and practical, there are opportunities in every part of the country.

The colleges, adult education centres and private establishments listed will be pleased to send details of courses available.

None of them cover the whole range of gardening activities in any single year, but many will respond to a demand for instruction on a specific subject.

City and Guilds have a scheme covering the following subjects:

The Lawn
Trees and Shrubs
The Rock Garden
Apples and Pears and Other Top
 Fruit
Small Greenhouse Management
Vegetable Growing
Garden Soils
Soft Fruit
The Water Garden
Vegetative Propagation
Flower Arranging

Small Greenhouse Food Crops
Garden Construction
The Flower Garden
Flowers and Plants Under Glass
Garden Design
Pests and Diseases
Indoor Gardening
Garden Machinery
Seed Propagation
The Plant
Organic Gardening
The Garden Nature Reserve

There are no educational requirements for those wishing to take any of these courses, and though the objective is that people who enrol will eventually take examinations for a 'Certificate in Gardening', those who don't aspire to academic qualifications don't have to take the exams, they can just go along and learn for their own enjoyment.

List of Centres offering courses leading to examinations for the City and Guild 'Certificate in Gardening':

Bedfordshire
Leighton Linslade
Community Colleges,
Van Dyke Road,
Leighton Buzzard,
Bedfordshire
LU7 8HS.
(Tel. 0525 735769)

Shuttleworth
Agricultural College,
Old Warden Park,
Biggleswade,
Bedfordshire
SG18 9DX.
(Tel. 076727 441)

Berkshire
Berkshire College of
Agriculture,
Hall Place,
Burchetts Green,
Nr Maidenhead,
Berkshire SL6 6QR.
(Tel. 0628 824444/5)

Buckinghamshire
Aylesbury College of
Further Education and
Agriculture,
Oxford Road,
Aylesbury,
Buckinghamshire
HP21 8PD.
(Tel. 0296 34111)

Denbigh School,
Cornwall Grove,
Bletchley,
Milton Keynes,
Buckinghamshire
MK3 7HU.
(Tel. 0908 366001)

Cambridgeshire
Cambridgeshire
College of Agriculture,
Newcommon Bridge,
Wisbech,
Cambridgeshire
PE13 2SJ.
(Tel. 0945 581024)

Cambridgeshire
College of Agriculture
and Horticulture,
Landbeach Road,
Milton,
Cambridge CB4 4DB.
(Tel. 0223 860701)

Cambridgeshire
College of Agriculture
and Horticulture
(Sawtry Centre),
Green End Road,
Sawtry,
Huntingdon,
Cambridgeshire
PE17 5UY.
(Tel. 0487 830222)

Impington Village
College,
Impington,
Cambridge CB4 4LX.
(Tel. 0223 232835)

The Manor
Community College,
Arbury Road,
Cambridge CB4 2JF.
(Tel. 0223 354937)

Cheshire
North Cheshire
College,
Padgate Campus,
Fearnhead,
Warrington WA2 0DB.
(Tel. 0925 814343)

Cleveland
Stockton-Billingham
Technical College,
Oxbridge Avenue,
Stockton,
Cleveland TS18 4QA.
(Tel. 0642 552101)

Cornwall
Horticultural
Education Office,
County Hall,
Truro TR1 3BA.
(Tel. 0872 74282)

Cumbria
Ullswater Centre,
Penrith,
Cumbria CA11 8PO.
(Tel. 0768 4120)

Devon
Bicton College of
Agriculture,
East Budleigh,
East Devon EX9 7BY.
(Tel. 0395 68353)

Durham
Durham College of
Agriculture and
Horticulture,
Houghall,
Durham DH1 3SG.
(Tel. 091 386 1351)

East Sussex
Agricultural College,
Plumpton,
Lewes,
East Sussex
BN7 3AG.
(Tel. 0273 890454)

Brighton College of
Technology,
Pelham Street,
Brighton BN1 4FA.
(Tel. 0273 685971)

Essex
Havering Technical
College,
Ardleigh Green Road,
Hornchurch,
Essex RM11 2LL.
(Tel. 040 24 55011)

Gloucestershire
College of Agriculture,
Hartpury House,
Hartpury,
Gloucester GL19 3BD.
(Tel. 045 270 258)

Greater Manchester
South Manchester
Community College,
Moor Road,
Wythenshawe,
Manchester
M23 9BQ.
(Tel. 061 902 0131)

Hampshire
Cricklade College,
Charlton Road,
Andover,
Hampshire SP10 1EJ.
(Tel. 0264 63311)

Institute of Adult,
Youth and Community
Education,
Argyle Centre,
Argyle Road,
Southampton
SO2 0BQ.
(Tel. 0703 334467)

Sparsholt College –
Hampshire,
Sparsholt,
Nr Winchester,
Hampshire
SO21 2NF.
(Tel. 096 272 441)

The Tertiary College,
Bishopsfield Road,
Fareham,
Hampshire
PO14 1NH.
(Tel. 0329 235631)

**Hereford and
Worcester**
Hereford College of
Agriculture,
Holme Lacey,
Hereford and
Worcester HR2 6LL.
(Tel. 0432 73316)

The Lacon Childe
School,
Love Lane,
Cleobury Mortimer,
Nr Kidderminster,
Hereford and
Worcester DY14 8PE.
(Tel. 0299 270312)

St Mary's RC High
School,
Lugwardine,
Hereford and
Worcester HR1 4DR.
(Tel. 0432 850755)

Hertfordshire
Capel Manor
Horticulture and
Environmental
Centre,
Bullsmoor Lane,
Waltham Cross,
Hertfordshire
EN7 5HR.
(Tel. 0992 763849)

De Havilland College,
The Campus,
Welwyn Garden City,
Hertfordshire
AL8 6AH.
(Tel. 0707 326318)

Isle of Wight
College of Arts and
Technology,
Medina Way,
Newport,
Isle of Wight PO30 5TA.
(Tel. 0983 526631)

Isles of Scilly
Isles of Scilly School,
St Marys,
Isles of Scilly TR21 0JZ.
(Tel. 0720 22538)

Kent
Canterbury College of
Technology,
New Dover Road,
Canterbury,
Kent LT1 3AJ.
(Tel. 0227 766081)

Hadlow College of
Agriculture and
Horticulture,
Hadlow,
Tonbridge,
Kent TN11 0AL.
(Tel. 0732 850551)

Lancashire
Adult Education Centre,
Old Grammar School,
Whalley,
Lancashire BB6 9RH.
(Tel. 0254 822717)

College of Technology,
Parsons Walk,
Wigan,
Lancashire WN1 2LY.
(Tel. 0942 494911)

Lancashire College of
Agriculture and
Horticulture,
Myerscough Hall,
Bilsborrow,
Preston PR3 0RY.
(Tel. 0995 40611)

Leigh College,
Marshall Street,
Leigh,
Lancashire
WN7 4HX.
(Tel. 0942 608811)

Oldham Community
Education Centre,
Chaucer Street,
Oldham,
Lancashire OL1 1BA.
(Tel. 061 652 3085)

HM Prison,
Kirkham,
Preston,
Lancashire PR4 2RA.
(Tel. 0772 684343)

Runshaw Tertiary
College,
Langdale Road,
Leyland,
Preston PR5 2DQ.
(Tel. 0772 432511)

Tameside College of
Technology,
Beaufort Road,
Ashton-under-Lyne,
Lancashire OL6 6NX.
(Tel. 061 330 6911)

London
Lambeth Adult
Education Institute,
Strand Centre,
Elm Park,
London SW2 2EH.
(Tel. 01-671 1300)

South Greenwich
Adult Education
Institute,
Haimo Road,
London SE9 6DZ.
(Tel. 01-850 3632)

Southwark Institute of
Adult Education,
Queen's Road Centre,
St Mary's Road,
London SE15 2EA.
(Tel. 01-639 1178)

Waltham Forest
College,
Forest Road,
Walthamstow,
London E17 4JB.
(Tel. 01-527 2311)

Merseyside
The Hugh Baird
College of
Technology,
Balliol Road,
Bootle,
Merseyside L20 7EW.
(Tel. 051 992 6704)

Southport College of
Art & Technology,
Mornington Road,
Southport,
Merseyside PR9 0TT.
(Tel. 0704 42411)

Wirral Metropolitan
College Vocation
Preparation Department,
Withens Lane,
Wallasey,
Merseyside
LA45 7LT.
(Tel. 051 639 8371)

Middlesex
Heston School,
Heston Road,
Heston,
Hounslow,
Middlesex TW5 0QR.
(Tel. 01-572 1931)

Norwood Hall
Institute of
Horticultural
Education,
Norwood Green Road,
Southall,
Middlesex UB2 4LA.
(Tel. 01-574 2261)

Spring Grove
Community Education
Centre,
Thornbury Road,
Isleworth,
Middlesex TW7 4HG.
(Tel. 01-568 3699)

Norfolk
Norfolk College of
Arts and Technology,
Tennyson Avenue,
Kings Lynn,
Norfolk PE30 2QW.
(Tel. 0553 761144)

North Yorkshire
Askham Bryan
College,
Askham Bryan,
York YO2 3PR.
(Tel. 0904 702121)

Craven College of
Adult Education,
High Street,
Skipton,
North Yorkshire
BD23 1JY.
(Tel. 0756 61411).

Harlow Car Gardens,
Ceag Lane,
Harrogate,
North Yorkshire
HG3 1QB.
(Tel. 0423 65418)

Nottinghamshire
North
Nottinghamshire
College of Further
Education,
Carlton Road,
Worksop,
Nottinghamshire
S81 7HP.
(Tel. 0909 473561)

Nottinghamshire
College of Agriculture,
Brackenhurst,
Southwell,
Nottinghamshire.
(Tel. 0636 812252)

Oxfordshire
College of Further
Education,
Northcourt Road,
Abingdon,
Oxfordshire OX14 1NN.
(Tel. 0235 21585)

Denman College,
Marcham,
Abingdon,
Oxfordshire OX13 6NW.
(Tel. 0865 391219)

North Oxfordshire
Technical College and
School of Art,
Broughton Road,
Banbury,
Oxfordshire OX16 9QA.
(Tel. 0295 52221)

Shropshire
The Grove School,
Stafford Street,
Market Drayton,
Shropshire TF9 1HF.
(Tel. 0630 2121)

Oswestry College,
College Road,
Oswestry,
Shropshire SY11 2SA.
(Tel. 0691 653067)

Somerset
Somerset College of
Agriculture,
Cannington,
Nr Bridgwater,
Somerset TA5 2LS.
(Tel. 0278 652226)

Yeovil College,
Ilchester Road,
Yeovil,
Somerset BA21 2BA.
(Tel. 0935 23921)

South Yorkshire
Barnsley College of
Technology,
Church Street,
Barnsley,
South Yorkshire
S70 2AN.
(Tel. 0226 299191)

Don Valley Institute of
Further Education,
Bessacarr/Stirling
Further Education
Centre,
Prospect Place,
Doncaster DN1 3QP.
(Tel. 0302 66896)

Rother Valley College
of Further Education,
Doe Quarry Lane,
Dinnington,
Nr Sheffield
S31 7NH.
(Tel. 0909 550550)

Surrey
East Surrey College,
Gatton Point,
Redhill,
Surrey RH1 2JX.
(Tel. 0737 772611)

Kingston Adult
Education Service,
North Kingston Centre,
Richmond Road,
Kingston-upon-
Thames,
Surrey KT1 1EU.
(Tel. 01-546 2121)

Merrist Wood College
of Agriculture and
Horticulture,
Worplesdon,
Nr Guildford,
Surrey GU3 3PE.
(Tel. 0483 232424)

Tyne and Wear
College of Agriculture,
Kirkley Hall,
Ponteland,
Newcastle upon Tyne
NE20 0AQ.
(Tel. 0661 860808)

Fence Houses YTS,
c/o YMCA,
Lambton Lane,
Fence Houses,
Houghton-le-Spring,
Tyne and Wear
DH4 6HB.
(Tel. 0783 856236)

North Tyneside
College of Further
Education,
Embleton Avenue,
Wallsend,
Tyne and Wear
NE28 9NL.
(Tel. 091 262 4081)

South Tyneside College,
St George's Avenue,
South Shields,
Tyne and Wear
NE34 6ET.
(Tel. 091 456 0403)

Springboard Training
Centre,
2nd Floor, Burdon House,
Burdon Road,
Sunderland SR1 0QB.
(Tel. 0783 791835)

Warwickshire
South Warwickshire
College of Further
Education,
The Willows,
Alcester Road,
Stratford-upon-Avon,
Warwickshire
CV37 9QR.
(Tel. 0789 66245)

Tile Hill College of
Further Education,
Tile Hill Lane,
Coventry CV4 9SU.
(Tel. 0203 694200)

Warwickshire College
of Agriculture,
Moreton Morrell,
Warwick CV35 9BL.
(Tel. 0926 651 367)

West Midlands
Hall Green Technical
College,
Cole Bank Road,
Birmingham B28 8ES.
(Tel. 021 778 2311)

Shelfield Community
School,
Broadway,
High Heath,
Pelsall,
Walsall,
West Midlands
WS4 1BW.
(Tel. 0922 685777)

Solihull College of
Technology,
Blossomfield Road,
Solihull,
West Midlands
B91 1SB.
(Tel. 021 705 6376)

West Sussex
Crawley College of
Technology,
College Road,
Crawley,
Sussex RH10 1NR.
(Tel. 0293 25686)

West Yorkshire
Adult Education
Centre,
Park Road Centre,
Batley,
West Yorkshire
WF17 5LP.
(Tel. 0924 472623)

Cleckheaton Adult
Education Centre,
The Town Hall,
Church Street,
Cleckheaton,
West Yorkshire
BD19 3RH.
(Tel. 0274 870125)

Wakefield CVS and
Diocese,
Bottomboat School,
Stanley,
Nr Wakefield,
West Yorkshire
WF3 4AY.
(Tel. 0924 828810)

Wiltshire
Kingdown
Comprehensive
School,
Woodcock Road,
Warminster,
Wiltshire BA12 9DR.
(Tel. 0985 215551)

Lackham College of
Agriculture,
Lacock,
Nr Chippenham,
Wiltshire SN15 2NY.
(Tel. 0249 656111)

Trowbridge Technical
College,
College Road,
Trowbridge,
Wiltshire BA14 0ES.
(Tel. 022 14 66241)

WALES

Coleg Glynllifon,
Clynnog Road,
Caernarvon,
Gwynedd LL54 5DU.
(Tel. 028 830261)

College of
Horticulture,
Northop,
Nr Mold,
Clwyd CH7 6AA.
(Tel. 035 286 861)

Mid-Glamorgan
College of Agriculture
and Horticulture,
Tregroes,
Pencoed,
Mid Glamorgan
CF35 5LG.
(Tel. 0656 860202)

Montgomery College
of Further Education,
Llanidloes Road,
Newtown,
Powys.
(Tel. 0686 622722)

South Glamorgan
Institute of Higher
Education,
Western Avenue,
Llandaff,
Cardiff,
South Glamorgan
CF4 2RD.
(Tel. 0222 551111)

SCOTLAND

Barony Agricultural
College,
Parkgate,
Dumfries DG1 3NE.
(Tel. 0387 86251)

Clinterty Agricultural
College,
Kinellar,
Aberdeenshire
A85 0TN.
(Tel. 0224 79393)

Moray College of
Further Education,
Hay Street,
Elgin,
Morayshire IV30 1JJ.
(Tel. 0343 3425)

**NORTHERN
IRELAND**

College of Further
Education,
Lurgan Road,
Portadown,
Craigavon,
Northern Ireland
BT63 5BL.
(Tel. 0762 337111)

**CHANNEL
ISLANDS**

Heches Herbs of
Guernsey,
Les Heches,
St Peter in the Wood,
Guernsey,
Channel Islands.
(Tel. 0481 63545)

Highlands College,
St Saviour,
Jersey,
Channel Islands.
(Tel. 0534 71800)

EIRE

Regional Technical
College,
Cork Road,
Waterford,
Eire.
(Tel. 051 75934)

For the really keen amateur gardener the Royal Horticultural Society runs courses for its 'General Examination in Horticulture'.

The following are the places to enquire for details:

ENGLAND

Avon
Norton Radstock
Technical College,
South Hill Park,
Radstock,
Bath BA3 3RW.
(Tel. 0761 33161)

Bedfordshire
Shuttleworth College,
Old Warden Park,
Biggleswade,
Bedfordshire
SG18 9DX.
(Tel. 0767 27441)

Berkshire
Berkshire College of
Agriculture,
Hall Place,
Burchetts Green,
Nr Maidenhead,
Berkshire SL6 6QR.
(Tel. 062 882 4444/6)

Buckinghamshire
Aylesbury College,
Department of
Agriculture and
Horticulture,
Hampden Hall,
Stoke Mandeville,
Aylesbury,
Buckinghamshire
HP22 5TB.
(Tel. 029 661 3391)

Cambridgeshire
Cambridgeshire Farm
College,
Landbeach Road,
Milton,
Cambridge CB4 4DB.
(Tel. 0223 860701)

Cheshire
Cheshire College of
Agriculture,
Reaseheath,
Nantwich,
Cheshire CW5 6DF.
(Tel. 0270 625131)

Cleveland
Stockton/Billingham
Technical College,
The Causeway,
Billingham,
Cleveland TS23 2DB.
(Tel. 0642 562101)

Cornwall
Cornwall College of
Further Education and
Higher Education,
Trevenson Road,
Pool,
Redruth,
Cornwall TR15 3RD.
(Tel. 0209 712911)

Cumbria
Cumbria College of
Agriculture and Forestry,
Newton Rigg,
Penrith,
Cumbria CA11 0AH.
(Tel. 0768 63791)

Dorset
Dorset College of
Agriculture,
Kingston Maurward,
Dorchester,
Dorset DT2 8PY.
(Tel. 0305 64738)

Durham
Durham College of
Agriculture and
Horticulture,
Houghall,
Durham DH1 3SG.
(Tel: 091 386 1351)

East Sussex
Brighton College of
Technology,
Centre for Horticulture,
Stanmer Park,
Brighton,
East Sussex BN1 9PZ.
(Tel. 0273 601678)

Plumpton Agricultural
College,
Lewes,
East Sussex BN7 3AE.
(Tel. 0273 890454)

Essex
Southend Adult
Education Centre,
Ambleside Drive,
Southend-on-Sea,
Essex SS1 2UP.
(Tel. 0702 610196)

Gloucestershire
Gloucestershire
College of Agriculture
and Horticulture,
Hartpury House,
Nr Gloucester
CL19 3BD.
(Tel. 0452 283)

Greater Manchester
South Manchester
Community College,
Wythenshawe Park
Centre,
Manor Road,
Wythenshawe,
Manchester
M23 9BQ.
(Tel. 061 902 0131)

Tameside College of
Technology,
Beaufort Road,
Ashton-under-Lyne,
Tameside,
Greater Manchester
OL6 6NX.
(Tel. 061 330 6911)

See also under
Lancashire

Hampshire
Farnborough College
of Technology,
Boundary Road,
Farnborough,
Hampshire
GU14 6SB.
(Tel. 0252 515511)

Highbury College of
Technology,
Cosham,
Portsmouth,
Hampshire
PO6 2SA.
(Tel. 0705 383131)

Sparsholt College –
Hampshire,
Sparsholt,
Winchester,
Hampshire
SO21 2NF.
(Tel. 096 272 441)

Hertfordshire
Callowland Adult
Education Centre,
Leavesden Road,
Watford,
Hertfordshire
WD2 5EF.
(Tel. 0923 55533)

Capel Manor
Horticultural and
Environmental
Centre,
Bullsmoor Lane,
Waltham Cross,
Hertfordshire
EN7 5HR.
(Tel. 0992 763849)

Isle of Wight
Isle of Wight College
of Arts and
Technology,
Medina Way,
Newport,
Isle of Wight
PO30 5TA.
(Tel. 0983 526631)

Kent
Canterbury College of
Technology,
New Dover Road,
Canterbury,
Kent CT1 3AJ.
(Tel. 0227 66081)

Lancashire
Lancashire College of
Agriculture and
Horticulture,
Myerscough Hall,
Bilsborrow,
Preston,
Lancashire PR3 0RY.
(Tel. 0995 40611)

Wigan College of
Technology,
Parsons Walk,
Wigan,
Lancashire WN1 1RR.
(Tel. 0942 494911)

See also under Greater
Manchester

London
Merton Institute of
Adult Education,
Whatley Avenue,
Wimbledon,
London SW20 9NS.
(Tel. 01-543 9292)

Sheen School,
Hertford Centre,
Hertford Avenue,
East Sheen,
London SW14.
(Tel. 01-876 8893)

South London
College,
Knights Hill,
London SE27 0TX.
(Tel. 01-670 4488)

Southwark College,
The Cut,
London SE1 8LE.
(Tel. 01-928 9561)

See also under
Middlesex and Surrey

Merseyside
Southport College of
Art and Technology,
Mornington Road,
Southport,
Merseyside PR9 0TT.
(Tel. 0704 42411)

Middlesex
Frays Adult Education
Centre,
65 Harefield Road,
Uxbridge,
Middlesex UB8 1PJ.
(Tel. 0895 54766)

North Hillingdon
Adult Education Centre,
86 Long Lane,
Ickenham,
Uxbridge,
Middlesex UB10 8SX.
(Tel. 089 56 34616)

Norwood Hall
Institute of Horticultural
Education,
Norwood Green Road,
Norwood Green,
Southall,
Middlesex UB2 4LA.
(Tel. 01-574 2261)

Rooks Heath High School,
Eastcote Lane,
South Harrow,
West Middlesex
HA2 9AG.
(Tel. 01-422 4675)

Whitton School,
Percy Road,
Whitton,
Middlesex TW2 6JW.
(Tel. 01-894 4503)

See also under London
and Surrey

Norfolk
Norfolk College of
Agriculture and
Horticulture,
Department of
Horticulture,
Burlingham,
Norwich NR13 4TA.
(Tel. 0603 712598)

North Yorkshire
Northern
Horticultural Society,
Harlow Car Gardens,
Crag Lane,
Harrogate,
North Yorkshire
HG3 1QB.
(Tel. 0423 65418)

Northamptonshire
Northamptonshire
College of Agriculture,
West Street,
Moulton,
Northampton
NN3 1RR.
(Tel. 0604 491131)

The Oundle Area
Adult Education
Centre,
Prince William
School,
Herne Road,
Oundle,
Peterborough.
(Tel. 0832 73550)

Northumberland
Northumberland
College of Agriculture,
Kirkley Hall,
Ponteland,
Newcastle upon Tyne
NE20 0AQ.
(Tel. 0661 24141)

Nottinghamshire
Nottinghamshire
College of Agriculture,
Brackenhurst,
Southwell,
Nottinghamshire
NG25 0QF.
(Tel. 0636 812252)

Oxfordshire
North Oxfordshire
Technical College and
School of Art,
Broughton Road,
Banbury,
Oxfordshire
OX16 9QA.
(Tel. 0295 52221)

Oxford University
Botany School,
South Parks Road,
Oxford OX1 3RA.
(Tel. 0865 275000)

Shropshire
Grove School,
Market Drayton,
Shropshire TF9 1HF.
(Tel. 0630 652121)

Horticultural
Education
Department,
Radbrook Centre,
Radbrook Road,
Shrewsbury SY3 9BL.
(Tel. 0743 60266)

Somerset
The School of
Agriculture and
Horticulture,
Yeovil College,
Ilchester Road,
Yeovil,
Somerset BA21 3BA.
(Tel. 0935 23921)

South Yorkshire
Rother Valley College
of Further Education,
Doe Quarry Lane,
Dinnington,
Sheffield S31 7NH.
(Tel: 0909 568681)

Suffolk
Otley College of
Agriculture and
Horticulture,
Otley,
Ipswich,
Suffolk IP6 9EY.
(Tel. 047 385 543)

Surrey
Kingston Adult
Education Service,
Room 19,
North Kingston
Centre,
Richmond,
Kingston-upon-
Thames,
Surrey KT2 5PE.
(Tel. 01-546 2121)

Mid-Surrey Adult
Education Institute,
Stoneleigh Centre,
Sparrow Farm Road,
Stoneleigh
KT17 2LW.
(Tel. 01-394 1333)

Royal Botanic
Gardens,
Kew,
Richmond,
Surrey TW9 3AB.
(Tel. 01-940 1171)

See also under
London and Middlesex

Tyne and Wear
North Tyneside
College of Further
Education,
Embleton Avenue,
Wallsend,
Tyne and Wear
NE28 9NJ.
(Tel. 091 2624081/3)

Warwickshire
South Warwickshire
College of Further
Education,
The Willows North,
Alcester Road,
Stratford-upon-Avon
CV37 9QR.
(Tel. 0789 66245)

Warwickshire College
of Agriculture,
Moreton Morrell,
Warwick CV35 9BL.
(Tel. 0926 651367)

See also under West
Midlands.

West Midlands
Stourbridge College,
Horticultural Unit,
Leasowes Park Nursery,
Leasowes Lane,
Halesowen,
West Midlands
B62 8QF.
(Tel. 021 550 0007)

Tile Hill College of
Further Education,
Tile Hill Lane,
Tile Hill,
Coventry CV4 9DX.
(Tel. 0203 461444)

See also under
Warwickshire

West Sussex
Brinsbury College of
Agriculture and
Horticulture,
Brinsbury,
North Heath,
Pulborough,
West Sussex RH20 1DL.
(Tel. 079 82 3832/3/4
& 5222)

West Yorkshire
Leeds Polytechnic,
The Main Building,
School of Education,
Beckett Park,
Leeds LS6 3QS.
(Tel. 0532 759061)

Ralph Thoresby High
School (Adult
Education),
Farrar Lane,
Leeds LS16 7NQ.
(Tel. 0532 670338)

Shipley College,
Exhibition Road,
Shipley,
West Yorkshire BD18 3JW.
(Tel. 0274 595731)

Wakefield District
College,
(Hemsworth Centre),
Science Sector,
Station Road,
Hemsworth,
Pontefract,
West Yorkshire WF9 4JP.
(Tel. 0977 611169)

West Park Evening
Centre,
West Park High
School,
Spen Lane,
Leeds LS16 5BE.
(Tel. 0532 756065)
(Mondays and
Tuesdays, 7.00pm–
9.00pm)

Wiltshire
Lackham College of
Agriculture,
Lacock,
Chippenham,
Wiltshire SN15 2NY.
(Tel. 0249 656111)

WALES
Mid-Glamorgan
College of Agriculture
and Horticulture,
Tregroes,
Pencoed,
Bridgend,
Mid Glamorgan
CF35 5LG.
(Tel. 0656 860202)

SCOTLAND
The Barony College,
Parkgate,
Dumfries DG1 3NE.
(Tel. 038 786 251/655/
677)

Department of
Horticulture,
Woodburn House,
Buchanan Drive,
Rutherglen G73 3PF.
(Tel. 041 647 6300)

Moray College of
Further Education,
Hay Street,
Elgin,
Morayshire IV30 2NN.
(Tel. 0343 3425)

Threave School of
Gardening,
Castle Douglas,
Dumfries and
Galloway DG7 1RX.
(Tel. 0556 2575)

**NORTHERN
IRELAND**
Belfast College of
Technology,
College Square East,
Belfast,
Northern Ireland
BT1 6DJ.
(Tel. 0232 227244)

**CHANNEL
ISLANDS**
Highlands College,
Horticultural and
Training Centre,
Trinity,
Jersey,
Channel Islands.
(Tel. 61252)

EIRE
Kildalton Agricultural
and Horticultural
College,
Piltown,
County Kilkenny,
Eire.
(Tel. 051 43105)

National Botanic
Gardens,
Glasnevin,
Dublin 9,
Eire.
(Tel. 001 377596)

In many areas local parks departments have demonstrations and courses, and local education authorities not in our lists may well put on lectures in gardening at evening classes.

The National Federation of Women's Institutes Home Economics Gardening Certificate might interest lady enthusiasts. Enquire from your local W.I.

Finally, various private establishments offer short courses, some of which are residential at weekends.

The list that follows is not comprehensive so keep an eye on the local papers' advertisements.

There is, of course, a sort of gardening mafia, so that enquiries at one study centre may well lead to information about another that provides just the course that you want.

Private establishments running courses on gardening and landscaping:

The English
Gardening School,
Chelsea Physic Garden,
66 Royal Hospital Road,
London SW3 4HS.

The Fortescue Garden
Trust Summer Schools,
Garden House,
Buckland
Monachorum,
Yelverton,
South Devon.

The Garden School,
Treasures of Tenbury
Ltd,
Burford House
Gardens,
Tenbury Wells,
Worcestershire
WR15 8HQ.

Peterborough College
of Adult Education,
Brook Street,
Peterborough.

Other gardening courses, particularly those given at weekends, are usually advertised in the RHS Journal, *The Garden*. One establishment frequently advertising is:

R. J. Mitchell, Esq,
Curator,
University Botanic
Garden,
St Andrews,
Fife KY16 8RT.

Other establishments offering gardening weekends and holidays in recent issues of the Journal and elsewhere are:

Chenies Manor
House,
Chenies,
Buckinghamshire.

The Coombe Cross
Hotel,
Bovey Tracey,
Devon.

Field Studies Council,
Flatford Mill Field Centre,
East Bergholt,
Colchester CO7 6UL.

The Gilbert White
Museum,
'The Wakes',
Selborne,
Alton,
Hampshire GU34 3JH.

Heches Herbs of
Guernsey,
Les Heches,
St Peter in the Wood,
Guernsey,
Channel Islands.

The Ironbridge
Institute,
Ironbridge Gorge
Museum,
Ironbridge,
Telford,
Shropshire TF8 7AW.

J.A.R. Services,
Garden House,
Tudor Close,
Thorpe Willoughby,
Selby YO8 9NP.

National Institute of
Adult Continuing
Education,
19B De Montford
Street,
Leicester LE1 7GE.

The Old Postern Short
Course Centre,
Dartington Tech Ltd,
Dartington,
Totnes,
Devon TQ9 6EA.

University Summer
School,
Contact: Carol
Williams,
Conference Office,
University College of
North Wales,
Bangor,
Gwynedd LL57 2DG.

West Kington
Nurseries,
Pound Hill House,
West Kington,
Wiltshire SN14 7JG.

Very occasionally horticultural courses are advertised for:

West Dean College,
West Dean,
Nr Chichester,
West Sussex
PO18 0QZ.

Earnley Concourse,
Nr Chichester,
Sussex PO28 7JL.

Weekend courses are held at Pershore College of Horticulture, Avonbank, Pershore, Worcestershire.

Courses on botany relating to the area are given at:

The Kingcombe
Centre,
Toller Porcorum,
Dorchester DT2 0EQ.

The Royal Horticultural Society have an up-to-date list of activities available from:

Miss Audrey V. Brooks,
The R.H.S. Garden,
Wisley,
Woking,
Surrey GU23 6QB.

GROW YOUR
♦ OWN GRUB ♦

A Sowing and Planting Guide for Vegetables

> **REDMOND RECOMMENDS** Titch Redmond, in his eightieth year, has rather more than a lifetime's gardening experience. Added to that, his father was a head gardener with a bent for rather unusual experiments, so a chat with Titch is punctuated with some very odd ideas. They are scattered throughout this chapter, together with some straightforward advice that is common knowledge, yet we tend to forget it.

♦ SOIL ♦

It bears repeating again and again that you will not grow good plants in bad soil. All soils from sandy to heavy clays, if tramped on, neglected and fertilised only by cats and dogs, become very tired. So you must rejuvenate by digging, at the same time incorporating muck or any sort of compost; failing that, moss peat raked into the top few inches of soil at 6½ lb/sq yd (3 kg/sq m) will get your plants started. There should be millions of bugs and bacteria in your garden soil. They all need air, and most of them feed on decaying vegetable matter: give them both and they'll multiply. They, and the plant roots, will turn any sort of bad soil into a good one in just a year or two.

A leaf bin (left) and
a compost bin (right)

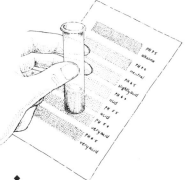

It is very important to know roughly how acid or alkaline the soil is. You can test it very easily – your garden centre will almost certainly have the very cheap Rapitest kit (*right*), which consists of a small test tube, powder and clear instructions.

◆ SEEDBED ◆

Seedlings and small plants have tiny roots, and these must be in contact with *small* soil particles. It's no good sowing or planting in lumpy, cobbly soil. Somehow with rake or hoe you must create what is known as a fine tilth: that is, the top few inches of soil must be thoroughly broken up.

On a heavy soil, at the pioneering stage, the aforementioned treatment with peat will help a lot.

◆ THE CALENDAR ◆

Just in case you compare our sowing dates with those in other books, and particularly if you live in the south, we should emphasise that our inclination to what is appropriate for northern climes is deliberate. Most of us have an insatiable urge to sow early – often too early. There is plenty of experimental evidence that later-sown crops catch up with their earlier brothers and sisters. No one has ever revived a seedling that's frozen.

Gardeners with heated greenhouses, propagators and enormous windowsills will, of course, be determined to start their sowing early. Those without, but equally keen to be ahead of the game, should seriously consider investment in cloches and sawn-off plastic lemonade bottles.

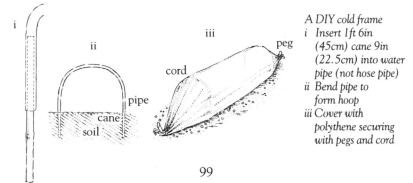

A DIY cold frame
i Insert 1ft 6in (45cm) cane 9in (22.5cm) into water pipe (not hose pipe)
ii Bend pipe to form hoop
iii Cover with polythene securing with pegs and cord

They can be in use throughout the year, and protect the seeds and seedlings from pests, cats, mice, birds and, to a high degree, slugs. However, when growing seeds and plants under cover in this way, beware of hot weather: make sure that they are well ventilated and shaded and that they do not 'cook'.

In all cases information given in the following pages, and that on the back of seed packets, pales in comparison with the advice of a gardening neighbour whose knowledge of your local climate and conditions is based on years of experience. So a guide it is, no more. Choose what you want to grow, check that it will flourish in your soil, discuss with Fred down the road, and pray for a good growing season.

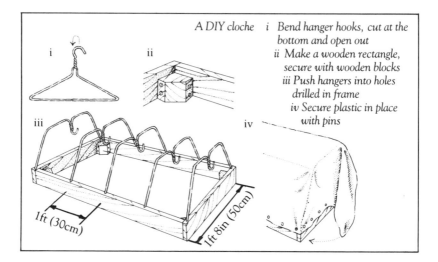

A DIY cloche
i Bend hanger hooks, cut at the bottom and open out
ii Make a wooden rectangle, secure with wooden blocks
iii Push hangers into holes drilled in frame
iv Secure plastic in place with pins

1ft (30cm)
1ft 8in (50cm)

• ROTATIONS •

We have grouped our vegetables into roots, brassicas and others to help you avoid diseases and pests. It really is important not to grow the same crop in the same place two or more years running; if you do, the pests and diseases that attack individual species build up. So divide your plot into three or four different sections, and sow from each group into a different area from year to year. Plot A grows roots in year one, then brassicas in year two, and others in years three and four. Plot B has roots in year two and so on.

YEAR 1	YEAR 2	YEAR 3
ROOTS	OTHERS	BRASSICAS
Potatoes	Peas	Cabbage
Swedes	Beans	Cauliflower
Turnips	Lettuces	Brussels sprouts
Carrots	Endives	Radishes
Parsnips		Kohl Rabi

REDMOND RECOMMENDS The lord of the manor sees to it that Titch gets as much 'bullock yard muck' as he wants, so he never uses Growmore or other inorganic fertilisers, except in the following instance: 'After you've sown and covered your seeds, scatter a few pellets, very thinly, of Nitrochalk or another high nitrogen fertiliser on top of the drill. The dew or a bit of rain will break them down and the shoots will grow and green up very quick.'

• ROOTS •

JERUSALEM ARTICHOKES

Plant in late March. Easy to grow.

Soil The Jerusalem artichoke is like the potato in almost every respect, except taste; it is a good pioneer crop. Dig in plenty of compost in autumn.

Position Will stand a bit of shade and, as the plants grow very tall – 5 ft (1.5 m) or more, planting a row next to the fence minimises the shading of other crops. And because, like parsnips, Jerusalem artichokes can winter in the ground, there is less interference with preparations for next year.

Varieties

The common old varieties are very knobbly, as if covered by warts large and small, so they are a nightmare in the kitchen. The new, much smoother-skinned 'Fuseau' is the one to buy.

Planting Set 5½ inches (14 cm) deep and 18 inches (45 cm) apart in the row, on a bit of peat if the soil is lumpy.

Cultivation One row is enough because Jerusalem artichokes need support: a post at each end and wires stretched between. They may need earthing up, and do need water in dry periods.

Fertiliser A generous handful of Growmore per sq yd well mixed in at planting time.

Difficulties Slugs and other creepy-crawlies love Jerusalem artichokes just as much as your editors. Watering with aluminium sulphate may discourage them from hollowing out the roots that you had intended to boil and butter for your own pleasure.

BEETROOT

Sow in April.

Soil Will grow in any soil which is not too acid (test and apply lime if necessary, well in advance of sowing). Ideally dig in rotted compost or rotted old manure in autumn. Lighter soils grow the best roots.

Position Beetroot like a sunny place.

Varieties

Globes These grow quickly and most don't bolt if sown earlyish. 'Boltardy' is a favourite. Choose others by browsing through the catalogue. There are white and yellow varieties which have the advantage that their leaves can be cooked as well as their roots.

Long These do need lighter soils and nowadays their main function is to win a prize at the village show.

Sowing Sow in rows 1 ft (30 cm) apart and ¾ inch (2 cm) deep. Put two or three seeds together in groups 4 inches (10 cm) apart and pull out the weakest when 1–2 inches (2.5–5 cm) high. The seeds have thick skins and take a while to germinate, usually 2 weeks; it's not a bad idea to soak them before sowing. Your editor has had no success at all with the multiple seed technique of growing in clumps of four or five. Geoff Hamilton thinks this is the sensible way to grow beetroot, especially on a small plot. But, of course, he's a good gardener with very good soil.

Try growing in groups of six in the flower border. They're decorative.

Succession of Crops Beetroot lovers sow a short row every 3 weeks or so right through until July.

Cultivation Beetroot is an easy crop to grow, not needing a very fine seedbed. Hoe the weeds away and water in dry spells. The roots grow woody if short of moisture.

Fertiliser In theory you should apply a handful of general-purpose fertiliser like Growmore per sq yd a week or two before sowing. If you forget, apply at sowing time and rake into the soil very thoroughly.

Difficulties Not many. Sown too early, beetroot may bolt – that is, throw up a seedhead rather than make a root. Your editor has achieved this with a bolt-resistant variety!

If the roots turn black in the middle, your soil may be over-limed and short of the trace element boron.

CARROTS

Sow in April.

Soil Carrots don't like heavy soils very much; they do best in light, sandy soils which have had plenty of compost or manure dug into them. However, they do not like fresh compost or manure, so leave these out of the carrot patch when you dig in autumn.

Position Sunny.

Varieties

Short These are mostly early. 'Kundulus' should be successful in heavier

> **REDMOND RECOMMENDS** If Titch sees any plant looking 'wrong', he doesn't hesitate: he pulls it up and burns it. Mildew, yellow leaves or wilting, out they come. If he removes a carrot, and sees a brown tip to the root, 'that's carrot fly, and I'll dig up the whole row; ten to one they've all got it.'

soils and is blunt-ended, a shape that seems to be the best choice in difficult conditions; 'Early Nantes' is the most popular. Study your catalogue.

Intermediate 'Autumn King' is stumpy in shape, yields well and is hardy; you can leave it in the soil all winter. 'Chantenay' is also blunt-ended and very popular.

Long Grow 'St Valery' for the show bench.

Sowing Sow in rows, or in clumps to reduce weeding (try the latter in the flower border). The seeds should go in *thinly* at a depth of just over ½ inch (1 cm).

Succession of Crops For really tender carrots throughout the summer, sow every 3 weeks. If that's too much bother, intermediate varieties can be cropped as they grow. Sow a short variety in August or even early September for your Christmas dinner.

Cultivation Carrots prefer to grow in ground that has undergone deepish digging in autumn with no compost or muck added. A fine tilth is necessary for sowing, though not too fine or the soil may cap (form a sort of tough skin on top after a heavy shower of rain). Thinning and weeding is best done by hand. Try not to bruise the foliage because the dreaded carrot fly will be attracted by the smell of broken carrot leaves. Earth up stubby varieties to stop the top of the root going green.

Fertiliser Rake in Growmore a week or so before sowing, and apply bromophos, as an anti-carrot fly insecticide, at the same time.

Difficulties Split roots are caused by irregular watering. Fanged roots can be caused by stones or overcompacted soil. Freshish compost or manure has the same effect.

The real enemy is the maggot of the carrot fly which feeds on the plant at every stage of growth. It will gobble up seedlings and riddle mature roots with holes. Defences against this pest are:

1 The bromophos treatment at sowing time.

2 A carrot cage which causes the female, when meeting the barrier, to fly up and over and on to your neighbour's carrots.

3 The Henry Doubleday researchers have come up with another organic way to confuse female carrot flies. Sow a row of carrots between eight rows of onions, four rows on either side. Three rows are not enough of a barrier, so you have to be fond of onions!

PARSNIPS

Sow in late March. Easy to grow, but there are some 'don'ts'.
Soil Any soil that has been well dug and isn't stony. As with carrots, don't
dig in compost and muck.
Position Will grow in light shade. Because it is in the ground for such a
long time, the growing season for a parsnip is an extended one.

Varieties

'Avonresister' and 'White Gem' are the best bets. They are resistant to
canker. Neither grows very big. 'Tender and True' and 'Cobham Improved
Marrow' are long and smooth and will catch a judge's eye, but they need
deep, light soil. Buy new seed every year.
Sowing Sow ½ inch (1 cm) deep in rows, and thin to 5 inches (12.5 cm)
between plants. Parsnips hate being moved, so forget about propagators,
windowsills and transplanting.
Cultivation To grow long roots prepare the soil by deep digging. When
hoeing to remove weeds, be very careful not to touch the crowns of the
roots or the dreaded canker will strike.
Fertiliser A handful of Growmore per sq yd, add lime to acid soil.
Difficulties Canker is the only real problem. The addition of water in dry
periods, lime to neutralise acid soil and *no* fresh compost or muck at
digging time should reduce the chances of root infection to very long odds.

Parsnips can stay in the ground all winter and taste better after being
frosted, especially roasted with the Sunday beef.

POTATOES

Plant in late March. Simple to grow well, but stick to the rules.
Soil Potatoes like acidity, so almost any soil will do apart from chalk. On
new ground reclaimed either from grass or the builders – they are *the*
pioneer crop. They prefer the soil to be prepared with a good, deep
autumn dig, incorporating as much compost or manure as is available.
Position Early potatoes need it sunny because the idea is that they should
grow fast; maincrop can stand a bit of shade, but do better in the open.

Varieties

There are dozens of varieties to choose from, but as most of us have only a
small plot, earlies, which are out of the ground by mid-July, making space
for another crop, are favourite. 'Arran Pilot', 'Epicure', 'Home Guard' and
'Duke of York' are all good oldies. 'Maris Bard' and 'Pentland Javelin' are
quick growers, and there are any number of newer varieties.

There are second early and maincrop varieties galore, their virtues
extolled in the seedsmen's brochures. To choose one you could close your
eyes and stick a pin in your catalogue, but make sure you buy certified seed

> *REDMOND RECOMMENDS* Titch claims that if you can get it, soot will keep wireworm, leatherjackets, slugs and other voracious creepy-crawlies at bay. For potatoes Titch applies soot down in the drill at planting time. 'The soot must be at least a year old before you use it,' says Titch.

(look at the label). Conservative, sour, boring, stick-in-the-mud, old gardeners recommend 'Arran Pilot' for earlies, 'Desirée' for maincrop.

Buy the seed in February and spread it out on a tray in a *light*, frost-free place. It will then chit (grow small, green shoots) which give a head start to an early crop. Don't leave seed in the dark: the tubers will grow long, white shoots that get knocked off at planting time.

Planting Plant earlies 5 inches (12.5 cm) deep at 1 ft (30 cm) intervals in rows which are 2 ft (60 cm) apart; plant maincrop a little deeper and more widely spaced. If the soil is really knobbly, encase them in a handful of peat before covering.

Cultivation When pioneering new ground, a deep dig and a real effort to break up all the bigger clods is important.

When the shoots show green on the surface, keep an ear open for frost warnings, then either cover with soil or compost. Hoe between rows for weeds at the early stage; after that the potato tops will smother them.

It is important to earth up the rows by some means, because potato tubers growing on the soil's surface turn green and are then poisonous.

Watering in dry weather is vital, especially when the tubers are forming in late May and June. Potatoes are around 90 per cent water.

Fertiliser Potatoes are greedy. At planting time spread a generous handful per sq yd of Growmore on the soil that you are about to put back on top of the seed. Then, as you fill in, the fertiliser will mix up well with the soil.

Difficulties Maincrop potatoes can suffer a profusion of ailments, most of which will not arise if the seed is certified and you stick rigidly to a rotation. Early varieties are less likely to suffer, but bugs, slugs and bacteria are always with us. If something looks wrong, put the diseased plant material in the dustbin (*not* on the compost heap), or burn it, and don't plant potatoes in the same place again for 3 or 4 years. But never be discouraged: new potatoes from your own garden are one of the joys of life.

◆ PEAS AND BEANS ◆
PEAS

It is possible to have crops of peas continuously from early May until October. However, with some of the very early and late sowings yields can be quite low, so we will concentrate here on main season growth.

Soil Peas like a soil that is not too acid and has enough humus to retain moisture. Poor soils give a disappointing crop.
Position In sun or light shade.

Varieties

Among the first earlies, 'Kelvedon Wonder' is one of the older tried-and-trusted peas that is a good cropper and can be sown in succession up to June for an autumn crop. For maincrop peas the best by far, if you have some room, is 'Alderman'. It is a plant that the Victorians knew and is still, in the editor's opinion, one of the best-flavoured varieties. Its only drawback is that it grows to about 5 ft (1.5 m) high, so you need to allow about the same distance between rows. It could be, of course, that one row would be enough to fill the freezer.

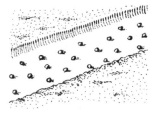

Sowing To sow first earlies take out a wide drill of about 8 inches (20 cm) wide and 2 inches (5 cm) deep. Spread seeds in the drill at about 2 inches (5 cm) apart in all directions. Sow in succession from late-March onwards. Sow maincrop peas as above from late April until early May.

Cultivation Apart from weeding, there is not a lot to do. Supporting the plants can be quite a test of your ingenuity, so you'll have to be inventive.

First earlies need staking up to about 2 ft (60 cm) and maincrop up to 5 ft (1.5 m).

Water well in dry spells when the pods begin to form.

Fertiliser Add an ounce of Growmore per sq yd a week before you sow.

Difficulties Not many. Keep the birds away from the emerging plants by covering with wire netting or lengths of black cotton. Pea and bean weevil may nibble around the edges of the leaves but will do little harm.

REDMOND RECOMMENDS Titch has his own variety of peas – goodness knows what their breeding is – and he saves seed every year. Very often they yield a dozen peas to the pod, and he's very proud of them. 'Never grow peas on the same ground; you must give them a 3-year gap.'

BROAD BEANS

Easy.
Soil Broad beans are happy in almost any free-draining soil.
Position Reasonably sunny.

Varieties

To avoid newcomers to gardening being disappointed, we have purposely left out autumn-sown broad beans as a hard winter can decimate a crop planted north of Watford. However, if you want to try, the 'Aquadulce' is the best bet. For spring sowing the 'Masterpiece Long Pod' or 'Green' or 'White Windsor' are favourites.

Sowing Best in a double row with 8 inches (20 cm) between each one and the seeds planted at 8 inch (20 cm) intervals, 2 inches (5 cm) deep. Sow when conditions let you in March or April and rake in a handful of Growmore to the sq yd a week before you sow.

Cultivation Not a lot to do. There is weeding, of course, and keeping an eye open for blackfly (see under 'Difficulties' below).

Fertiliser Add an ounce of Growmore per sq yd a week before you sow.

Difficulties Blackfly are particularly fond of broad beans. As soon as the pods begin to form, pinch out the top 3 inches (7.5 cm) of the plants and cook the trimmings as you would spinach. Thus you will not only deter the dreaded aphid, but you will also experience a different and delicious dish.

FRENCH BEANS

Soil Be reasonably generous to the soil with whatever humus-forming material you can lay your hands on and apply a good handful of Growmore per sq yd about 2 weeks before sowing time.

Position Reasonably sunny and sheltered spot.

Varieties

'Prince' is a very popular variety, but for a change try 'Pros' – this can be picked very young when only about 2–3 inches (5–7.5 cm) long, cooked very quickly and eaten with relish.

Sowing French beans can be sown under glass in April and planted out under cloches for an early crop. Most gardeners, however, avoid the problem of frost by sowing outside at the end of May in rows 18 inches (45 cm) apart, leaving about 4 inches (10 cm) between each seed. As with all the peas and beans, they should be sown 2 inches (5 cm) deep. You can sow French beans in succession up till the end of June.

Cultivation Watch out for slugs (see page 29) and keep the beans free of weeds. You need to devise some system of support for the taller-growing varieties as they can fall over with a heavy crop. Keep picking them as soon as they are ready.

Fertiliser Add an ounce of Growmore per sq yd a week before you sow.

Difficulties Again, blackfly can be tiresome, so spray with some environmentally friendly insecticide like pyrethrum.

Lack of water, especially when the pods are forming, is likely to lead to a disappointing crop, so water well in dry periods.

RUNNER BEANS

Soil For runner beans preparation is everything, so when you have time in the autumn or early spring and the soil is easy to deal with, dig out a trench a yard across by however long you want the row and at least a foot deep. Loosen the soil in the bottom of the trench with a fork, half-fill it with mushroom compost, garden compost or well rotted manure, pile the soil back on top and leave it to settle. (To keep the weeds at bay until it is time to plant, cover with black polythene.) Runner beans need a moisture-retentive soil and a good, deep root run.

Position Sunny and not too exposed to the wind.

Varieties

Again, the old ones are worth a try. 'Scarlet Emperor' takes some beating. For long pods 'Enorma' is a good bet and also has an excellent flavour.

Support Make an archway of poles or canes, two rows of them 18 inches (45 cm) apart with the poles 9 inches (22.5 cm) apart in the row. Tie the poles where they cross at the top and also tie in an extra long pole along the top where the poles cross (*right*). When the beans are fully grown, they produce quite a sail area with which high winds can create havoc, so make sure that each vertical pole is firmly inserted at least 6 inches (15 cm) into the soil. Another precaution is to tie extra poles diagonally along the rows.

Sowing Don't be hasty wait for May. Plant one seed 2 inches (5 cm) deep at the bottom of each cane and sow a few more at the end of the row to replace any duds you may find.

Cultivation Not a lot to do except for weeding and watering in dry weather when the pods have formed.

Fertiliser Add an ounce of Growmore per sq yd a week before you sow.

Difficulties Sometimes runner beans are reluctant to form pods at first. We have received many tips on how to overcome this problem, but none of them seems to work. The pods do form eventually and will produce more than enough for your needs, so do not worry.

Blackfly is the monster you have to look out for. We do not recommend you pick them off individually as life is too short. Be cautious about using sprays and use only those that are deemed safe.

AFTERWARDS

Peas and beans can all convert nitrogen from the air into a useable form, so when cropping has finished dig in the plants to provide a good green manure.

◆ SALADS ◆
ENDIVES

Soil A good, humus-rich soil that is not too heavy is best.
Position Sun or light shade.

Varieties
Broad-leaved 'Batavian Green' is good but better are the curly-leaved 'Moss Curled' or 'Green Curled'.
Sowing For the curly endive, sow between May and August; for the broad-leaved type, sow between July and September for a winter crop.

Sow in drills 1 ft (30 cm) apart and ½ inch (1 cm) deep. Water each drill, sow as thinly as you can and cover with dry soil.
Cultivation Thin the seedlings when the first true leaves appear to about 9 inches (22.5 cm) apart for curly-leaved varieties and 12 inches (30 cm) apart for broad-leaved.

Hoe the weeds regularly and water well in dry weather.
Fertiliser Add an ounce of Growmore per sq yd a week before you sow.
Blanching If you prefer the slightly bitter flavour of endive, there is no need to blanch. However, for those who prefer a milder flavour, this is what you do. Twelve weeks after sowing, loosely tie up the leaves and cover them with a pot, bucket or something that will keep the light out. They should be blanched in about 3 weeks.
Difficulties Slugs (see page 29) and bolting – due to dry weather, so keep them well watered.

LETTUCES

Soil Lettuces need a soil with some organic matter in it, and it should have a little lime added if it is acid. Work up a good, fine tilth before you even think of sowing. Rake in Growmore a fortnight before sowing.
Position Sun or light shade.

Varieties
In any seed catalogue there are pages of lettuce varieties, so let us just divide them up and concentrate on a few.
Butterhead
Quick to mature in most soil conditions. Try 'Buttercrunch' and 'Continuity'.
Cos
Very crisp; has the best flavour. Try 'Little Gem' or 'Paris White'.
Crisphead
You get a lot of lettuce for your money, but not a lot of flavour. 'Iceberg' is a popular variety; 'Lollo Rossa' has reddish brown leaves.

Looseleaf
Cut-and-come-again lettuce with not a bad flavour. 'Salad Bowl' and 'Red Salad Bowl' are both worth trying.

Sowing For all lettuce the rule is do not sow too deep: they need light to germinate. Take out a drill ½ inch (1 cm) deep and water the drill. Sow thinly and cover with dry soil. Succession is the name of the game if you are not to have fifty lettuces all maturing at the same time. Remember that if you sow only half a row, you can thin it out and transplant the seedlings in the other half and the second half will mature about a fortnight later. Sow between mid-March and mid-July.

Cultivation Thin the seedlings as soon as the first true leaves show themselves, and transplant them if you have the room. The plants should finish up about 1 ft (30 cm) apart. Looseleaf lettuce needs only about 6 inches (15 cm) between plants.

Fertiliser A little bit of nitrogen during the growing season will give tardy plants a boost. A dusting of dried blood round the plant will be quite sufficient.

Difficulties Slugs (see page 29) and aphids. If you do not want to spray for the latter, all we can say is that it is easier to rinse them off cos lettuce than the more crinkly types.

◆ *BULBS* ◆

GARLIC

Easy to grow and very worth while financially. The editor worked out that his 10 yard row produced £50 worth of garlic at supermarket prices.

Soil Garlic will grow in any soil that is not too heavy and that has been manured a few months before planting.

Position Garlic loves the sun.

Varieties

Go to the supermarket and pick a bulb with the biggest cloves – it will be cheaper than buying from a seedsman.

Planting To grow really big bulbs, garlic should be planted late October or early November so that it can get its roots into the soil before the winter. Plant 6 inches (15 cm) apart in rows 1 ft (30 cm) apart or, if you have no room in the vegetable patch, dot them around the back of the flower border. Each clove should be planted 2 inches (5 cm) deep.

Cultivation Like all bulbs, garlic requires hand weeding, but otherwise little else needs to be done.

Fertiliser Add an ounce of Growmore per sq yd a week or so before planting.

Difficulties A tendency to rot in waterlogged soil.

Harvesting Lift when the leaves turn yellow and thoroughly dry off before tying in bunches and storing in a cool, dry, frost-free place.

LEEKS

Forget about the giants grown in the North-East. To grow these you need to live among flat caps, white scarves and whippets.

Soil Any untrodden soil that is not waterlogged.

Position Open and sunny.

Varieties

'Musselburgh' is an old favourite, but the new variety 'Autumn Mammoth-Snowstar' gives better results.

Sowing and Planting Sow under glass in February and prick out into boxes of compost at the loop stage. Plant outside in April or when they are about the length and thickness of a pencil. With a dibber make holes about 6–7 inches (15–17.5 cm) deep, 6 inches (15 cm) apart in rows 1 ft (30 cm) apart. Drop the plants into the holes and water in. Don't fill the holes with soil. If you must sow outside do it in April.

Cultivation The soil should have been well dug beforehand and kept loose and friable until planting. Like other bulbs, leeks do not like competition from weeds, so hand weeding is the order of the day.

Fertiliser A handful of Growmore per sq yd is all you need, unless you are growing pot leeks in the North-East and you have a magic potion consisting of Newcastle Brown Ale and bats' droppings.

Difficulties The humble leek has few enemies, so don't worry.

ONIONS

Soil Any good soil with free drainage is suitable. For the show bench you need to increase the fertility of the soil with well-rotted compost.

Position Best in an open and sunny place.

Varieties

From sets: Dobies' 'All Rounder' (these have kept in good condition through to the following April). *From seed:* for big show onions try 'Lancastrian'; for keeping look no further than 'Bedfordshire Champion'.

Planting Sets Planting sets is an easy way to grow very good onions for kitchen use. Cut off the tassels on the top of the sets to deter worms from getting a good hold and dragging them round the garden. (Everybody says it's the birds that do this, but when onion sets have been covered with birdproof net the sets still seem to turn themselves upside down during the night.) Using a trowel, bury the sets up to their shoulders at the same distance apart as for seedling onions. Growmore raked in a week before will work wonders.

Sowing and Planting For really big show onions sow under glass in January. When at the loop stage, prick out into large seedtrays filled with a good compost and, apart from watering, forget them until mid-March. Harden them off and plant out 4 inches (10 cm) apart in rows 9 inches (22.5 cm) apart. Sow seed outside in late-March.

A handful of Growmore per sq yd raked in a week or so before you plant will get them established quickly.

Cultivation Dig in some well-rotted manure when preparing the ground, but remember that overdoing the manure and fertiliser can lead to very thick-necked onions and can affect the keeping quality.

Onions adore the personal touch, so stick to hand weeding: hoeing can damage the roots and bulbs.

Fertiliser A handful of Growmore per sq yd a week or so before planting.

Difficulties Bolting can be a problem – that is, when plants throw up a flower stalk. It's usually due to too-early sowing or planting. Bulbs splitting at the base usually occurs after watering or heavy rain following a drought. Split bulbs will not keep very long in store. There are many other pests and diseases that onions can get, but these are unlikely to ruin the whole crop. Always burn diseased bulbs.

Harvesting When the foliage turns yellow, lift the onions with a fork on a dry day. Continue to dry them out in the greenhouse, or outdoors provided the weather is dry. After about 2 or 3 weeks, tie them to strings and hang them in a dry, cool, frost-free place. Check them every so often and throw any doubtful ones away.

SHALLOTS

Easy.
Soil Any good soil with free drainage.
Position Sunny, open spot.

Varieties

'Dutch Yellow' is a good cooking shallot, but often flat-sided. 'Hative de Niort' produces a brown-skinned, handsome bulb that is good for cooking, pickling and, because it tends to be larger, for showing off to your friends.

Planting Plant 6 inches (15 cm) apart in rows 9 inches (22.5 cm) apart in April. If planted too early, they tend to bolt. A handful of Growmore per sq yd will help them along.

Cultivation Apart from weeding, leave them alone until it is time to harvest.

Fertiliser A handful of Growmore per sq yd a week or so before planting.

Harvesting Lift the bulb clusters when the leaves have turned yellow in July. Separate the bulbs and leave to dry thoroughly before storing them in nets or old tights in a cool, dry, frost-free place.

SPRING ONIONS AND PICKLING ONIONS

Soil Good, friable soil with a fine tilth.
Position Sunny or lightly shaded.

Varieties

Spring: 'White Lisbon'; pickling: 'The Queen'.

Sowing Spring onions in late-March, pickling in May. Take out a drill ½ inch (1 cm) deep and water the drill. Sow seeds thinly and cover with dry soil.

Cultivation Weeding around spring onions has to be done with some care as there is a tendency to pull up the seedlings as well. It is wisest to leave weeding until after rainfall when the weeds come out more easily.

Fertiliser A handful of Growmore per sq yd a week or so before planting.

Difficulties Poor germination: this is usually due to inadequate soil preparation and poor tilth or sowing when the ground is too wet or cold.

Harvesting We always refer to 'pulling' spring onions. Quite often this means breaking off a few green leaves and leaving the onions in the ground. However, it's better to ease the entire plant out with a hand fork. Leave pickling onions until they have formed nice, round bulbs the size of a large marble.

♦ *BRASSICAS* ♦

'Eat up your greens' is an exhortation heard in childhood that should echo throughout our lives: the majority of the health-giving green vegetables are members of the cabbage family. If you want to grow a good crop, it is vital to follow the rules.

Difficulties Problems can be legion if you don't rotate brassica crops, avoid acidity and have well-firmed soil.

Clubroot is the most universal destroyer. This is a soil-borne disease, and infection can be tramped all over the garden if mud clings to your wellies. You can take precautions by not buying in small plants (and disease) from elsewhere; instead, always grow your own from seed. Dipping the roots of transplants in a benomyl solution possibly helps to keep clubroot at bay, and earthing up plants with damaged roots will result in some sort of crop (they grow roots from higher up the stem). But the best rule, at the first suspicion of infection, is to lift the plant with as much soil on the roots as possible, and burn the lot.

Weevils, mildews and spotting leaves, aphids and grubs and trace element deficiencies are a frightening host of enemies but fairly rare. The most comon are easy to deal with: caterpillars die between finger and thumb or underfoot; snails and slugs can be controlled by various means (see page 32); and if you're plagued by pigeons, hang a dinner gong outside the back door and give it a bang every time you see one.

113

GREEN SPROUTING BROCCOLI
(Calabrese)

Sow in late March under a cloche, because the earlier the crop, the better.
Soil Any soil with plenty of compost or manure incorporated is suitable, best dug in in autumn to allow it to settle firmly. It must not be acid (light green on your Rapitest soil test chart).
Position Sunny positions for both the nursery bed and the final planting area are best; the nursery bed should not be shaded.

Varieties

Calabrese is the late summer/autumn form of sprouting broccoli. If this editor were restricted to growing only one vegetable in the garden, calabrese would be it.

The very early varieties tend to grow one big cauliflower-like head and not much else, which is fine for the market gardener, but this grower wants to pick a panful of small heads twice a week for as many months as possible. Look very carefully at the seed packet before you buy.

'El Centro' goes on and on producing side shoots. 'Corvet' does grow a cauliflower head, but if you harvest it when small, the side shooting is quite vigorous. 'Early Romanesco' is in fact rather late in cropping (November) but delicious (as indeed they all are); it is a big-headed variety.

Sowing The nursery bed will probably be just one short row, because there isn't room in most gardens for more than twenty plants at most. Sow ½–¾ inch (about 1½ cm) deep, and thin out when the seedlings are ¾ inch (2 cm) high to leave a plant every 3½ inches (8 cm) or so.

Transplanting Transfer from the nursery bed when the plants are about 5 inches (12 cm) high. Water them at least an hour before lifting and dibble in in rows at least 1 ft (30 cm) apart with 8 inches (20 cm) between plants. The less time between lifting from the nursery bed and planting, the better. Make a small, muddy pool in the planting area and stir the roots in it before dropping the plant in the hole. Don't forget the rhubarb!

Cultivation Dig well in autumn is the theory, but if you find yourself way behind schedule and a rotovator is to hand, work the soil as deeply as you can, and when planting out, firm with the boot before sticking the dibber in, and again after planting. (Don't overdo it if the soil is dampish, though.) Always water in the plants, however moist the soil is.

It is easy to hoe between the plants, so do this frequently.

Fertiliser Rake a generous handful of Growmore per sq yd into the soil before firming and planting. Dust with bromophos at the same time to minimise cabbage root fly damage.

Spread lime to neutralise acid soils well in advance of planting – when sowing in the nursery is a good time, because it may need some as well.

A sprinkling of nitrogen fertiliser in late June accelerates growth.

PURPLE SPROUTING BROCCOLI

Sow early May.

Soil. Soil should be well composted, well dug and well firmed. Add lime if necessary.

Position Sunny and sheltered for the nursery bed, fairly sunny for the planting area.

Varieties

'Early Purple Sprouting' is very hardy and good in heavy soil in cold areas (it matures by March). 'Late Purple' may not be ready till later, but is an excellent pick-and-come-again type.

Sowing Sow ½–¾ inch (about 1½ cm) deep in a well-firmed nursery bed. Thin at ¾ inch (2 cm) high to 3½ inches (8 cm) apart.

Transplanting Transplant about 16 inches (40 cm) apart in rows, leaving the same distance between rows. (See under 'Calabrese' for planting tips.)

Cultivation As for calabrese. If the site is exposed, plants may need a cane for support. A firming boot around the bottom of stems loosened by wind or frost keeps the roots in intimate contact with the soil.

Fertiliser As for calabrese. Sprinkle on a little extra Growmore in July or August, but *not* high nitrogen fertiliser.

CABBAGES

If you are prepared to commit a large part of your garden to cabbages, you can eat some every day of the year. If not, think carefully and choose summer or autumn and/or spring types.

Soil The soil should be well dug and well firmed, but don't dig in fresh manure or poorly rotted compost. Acid soil needs lime.

Position Not too shady.

REDMOND RECOMMENDS Titch doesn't have a problem if all his cabbages look as if they will mature at the same time; he holds a few back. 'Stick a screwdriver through the stem, just below the bottom leaves, and shove a matchstick in the hole. They'll never go to seed. Seen 'em last two years!'

SUMMER CABBAGE

Sow in late March in a nursery bed.

Varieties

'Hispi', 'Greyhound' and 'Primo' are excellent, 'Derby Day' can be ready to cut on the day after which it is named (if sown in late February in a propagator or heated greenhouse) and 'Quicksleep' will mature and keep in the ground for several weeks without splitting. 'Wiam' is excellent for coleslaw.

Sowing Sow about ½ inch (1 cm) deep in the nursery bed. When covering, firm well with the back of the rake. Thin seedlings to 3½ inches (8 cm) apart.

Transplanting Seedlings should have six leaves before being moved. Water an hour before lifting from the nursery bed. Make a muddy puddle next to the planting area and stir the roots in it before dropping into the dibbled hole. Firm well and water in.

Cultivation Dig well, adding lime if necessary, but no fresh manure or compost. Keep the weeds down with the hoe.

Fertiliser A good handful of Growmore should be raked in per sq yd before you firm the ground for transplanting. Don't forget a dusting of bromophos at the same time – it is good damage control against the cabbage root fly.

RED CABBAGE

Sow at the end of April.

Varieties

'Red Dutch' ('Niggerhead') doesn't grow too large and so is good for the small plot (and pickling). You can eat 'Ruby Ball' from August to the new year.

Sowing, Transplanting, Fertiliser As for summer cabbage.

WINTER CABBAGE

Sow in May.

Varieties

'Celtic' and 'January King', strains of Savoy-type cabbages, will both keep in the ground for 2 months or more. 'Polinius', not quite so weather-hardy, is very good for a winter salad. 'Holland Winter White Extra Late' is another – cut and store hung upside down in a cool, frost-free place when mature.

Sowing and Transplanting Sow ½ inch (1 cm) deep in a nursery bed, and thin the seedlings to 3½ inches (8 cm). Transplant further apart than summer cabbage – allow about 18 inches (45 cm) between plants and between rows.

Cultivation and Fertiliser As for summer cabbages. Put a foot over the roots to firm after frost.

REDMOND RECOMMENDS **When harvesting spring cabbage, try not to disturb the root and cut just below the leaves. 'We used to cut a cross on the top of the stem, and the plant would grow three or four more little cabbages in the next 2 or 3 weeks.' Titch seems to regard the 'foreign' cut-and-come-again vegetables with much less enthusiasm.**

SAVOY CABBAGE

The crinkly cabbage; grow as the winter types.

Varieties

Choose 'Savoy King' for a big family: this variety can grow very large and will be ready to cut well before Christmas. Sow early to cut in September. 'Spivoy' can mature as early as 'Hispi' if sown at the same time. It can also be grown as a spring cabbage.

SPRING CABBAGE

Sow in a nursery bed in late July and August (it is a very good succession crop after early potatoes, early carrots and so on).

Varieties

'Durham Early' is hardy and reliable, as is 'Spring Hero', which has a round rather than cone-shaped head. 'April' matures very early in spring. If your ground is not clear of a previous crop until September, sow 'Offenham Wintergreen' directly into the ground in which it will mature.

Transplanting Spring cabbage is planted much closer than other types: allow 7 inches (18 cm) between plants and 9½ inches (24 cm) between rows.

Fertiliser Do *not* apply Growmore. There should be enough plant food left from the previous crop. The idea is that spring cabbage should grow slowly so that it withstands the winter cold.

Do not forget to lime the soil if the crop follows acid lovers like potatoes.

CAULIFLOWERS

Rather like the cabbage, the cauliflower is divided into three groups, summer, autumn and winter types.

Soil Cauliflowers do best on good soil, with plenty of manure or compost in it. If your soil is not up to much, it is better not to attempt growing them until you've improved it.

Position Cauliflowers like sun, and the winter varieties will appreciate a little shelter.

SUMMER CAULIFLOWER

Make or buy a cold-frame (see page 22) and get an early crop by sowing in October in the frame.

Varieties

'Snow Crown' is comparatively early if sown in a nursery bed in early April, and it doesn't grow too large. 'Alpha Polaris' can be sown at the same time or in the frame in autumn – a good variety for not-so-marvellous soil. 'Montano' is popular with market gardeners: October sowings are eatable in early June.

Sowing Sow about ½ inch (1 cm) deep in a cold-frame or nursery bed. Thin to 3½ inches (8 cm) when 1¼ inches (3 cm) tall.

October-sown plants in the cold-frame can be potted individually in 3 inch (7.5 cm) pots and placed back in the frame instead of being thinned. (Beware of the effects of frost on potted cauliflowers.)

Transplanting Earlies in the cold-frame, whether in the soil or a pot, should be moved in late April to rows 1 ft (30 cm) apart with 1 ft (30 cm) between plants (cloched if possible).

Moved at the six-leaf stage, the spring-sown plants need careful handling. Water at least an hour before lifting and keep as much soil on the roots as possible. Don't knock them about in muddy puddles. And you must always remember to dig a hole with a trowel rather than dropping them into a dibbed hole.

Cultivation The soil must be really firm. Cauliflowers are not easy to grow because they will curd (produce tiny cauliflowers) much too early if their growth is checked. Hence be very careful not to nudge them with the hoe, and in any dry spell, however short, give them water.

Fertiliser A handful of Growmore per sq yd (and treatment with bromophos) before or at planting is not enough. The hungry cauli likes a booster handful per sq yd in early July.

MINI CAULIFLOWER

Your editor has a soft spot for the mini cauliflower because of a run of success with the variety 'Garaut'. The mature heads are around 5½ inches (14 cm) in diameter, the perfect size for a family of four.

Sowing Sow where they will mature in rows 6 inches (15 cm) apart. Thin seedlings to 6 inches (15 cm). Don't sow too early: not before mid-April, and then under a cloche for safety; after that sow another row towards the end of May, and yet another in June.

AUTUMN CAULIFLOWER

Sow in May.

Varieties

'All the Year Round' is flexible as to sowing date, but not as quick to mature as the summer types. 'Tornia' will crop in September; 'Autumn Giant' in November. 'Barrier Reef' and 'Canberra', good, compact varieties that grow the right way up, are ready in October.

Sowing, Transplanting, Cultivation and Fertiliser As for summer varieties.

WINTER CAULIFLOWER

Sow in May. Winter cauliflowers are not easy to grow, they take up their ground for a very long time and, in your editor's opinion, do not taste as good as purple sprouting broccoli.

Varieties

'Purple Cape' is, as its name suggests, purple in the ground but turns a disappointing green in the pan. It crops in March, as does 'Early Feltham'. 'Walcheren Winter – Armado April' is not ready till April, neither is 'St George'.

Sowing, Transplanting, Cultivation and Fertiliser As for the summer and autumn types.

CURLY KALE

Sow in early May.

Soil Much more tolerant than other brassicas, kale will grow in just about any soil, so long as it doesn't get waterlogged. If it follows another early crop, which is sensible, there's no need to dig.

Position A little sun is highly desirable, and shelter from wind.

Varieties

If you are not familiar with this vegetable, grow 'Pentland Brig' and cook the tender leaves like spring cabbage in November/December (avoid letting them grow large, tough and bitter), then the succulent shoots will appear from February onwards rather like sprouting broccoli. 'Dwarf Green' is the variety for leaf and for a small garden. The other varieties are probably best fed to cows.

Sowing Sow in a seedbed about ½ inch (1 cm) deep. Thin to 3½ inches (8 cm).

Transplanting When you transplant will depend on when you've cleared the bed of the preceding early potatoes, carrots, peas or whatever. Don't leave it too late or the plants in the seedbed will grow long and leggy (no later than mid-July). Plant 14 inches (35 cm) apart both ways.

Cultivation Just clean up after the preceding crop and consolidate. Firm after frost. Keep weeds down with the hoe.

Fertiliser Rake in a handful of Growmore per sq yd before planting, and some lime if necessary. A liquid fertiliser in early spring, when the plants may look a bit sad, will encourage further growth.

KOHL RABI

Sow in May, June or July.

Soil Kohl rabi likes sandy conditions, but plenty of compost and manure dug in in autumn will lighten any type of soil. It will tolerate shallow soil.

Position A sunny spot.

Varieties

There are 'Green Vienna, 'Purple Vienna' and 'White Vienna', but they are put in the shade by 'Rowel'.

The root can be grated into salads raw, but is usually served boiled or braised. If harvested at tennis-ball size, the tops can be treated like spinach. Kohl rabi will stay in the ground until December.

Sowing Sow in a nursery bed ½ inch (1 cm) deep. Thin to 3½ inches (8 cm).

Transplanting Water the seedlings an hour before lifting. They should be 5 inches (12 cm) high before transplanting to 10 inches (25 cm) apart with 14 inches (35 cm) between rows.

Cultivation and Fertiliser Add lime if the soil is acid. Kohl rabi is a brassica, so bromophos should go on at the same time as the Growmore and be raked in before planting.

Hoe out weeds, water in dry spells, and bang a gong to keep the pigeons away.

RADISHES

Sow March to August.

Soil Very nearly any soil will do, but because the radish is a brassica, firm soil and non-acid conditions are, in theory, the essentials.

Position Radish will grow in any little patch that is unoccupied, but summer crops need shade, so a space in the flower border is practical.

Varieties

'Ribella', 'Cherry Belle' and 'French Breakfast' are good varieties.

Winter radish can stay in the ground until required – 'China Rose' is a favourite. 'Black Spanish Round' grows to turnip size, and you can boil it for Christmas dinner if your digestion is not already likely to suffer overstrain.

Sowing Sow ½ inch (1 cm) deep and thin to avoid desperate over-crowding. Winter varieties need at least 6 inches (15 cm) between plants.

Cultivation and Fertiliser Clear the weeds and stir the top soil with the rake for catch crop sowings. Firm the seed into place. Seedlings need a dust of powder or a spray against flea beetle.

A sprinkle of Growmore is a good idea for earlies. Winter crops will do better with some compost dug in as well.

BRUSSELS SPROUTS

Sow in April.

Soil Brussels sprouts prefer well-dug soil with plenty of manure and compost. Add lime if the soil is acid. Firm.

Position Sunnyish, and sheltered or they may blow over.

Varieties

'Peer Gynt' is a good autumn cropper sold by every seedsman. 'Widgeon' is resistant to mildew and rot, 'Welland' produces the biggest sprouts, but 'Predora' is the one for Christmas dinner and it also freezes well. 'Fortress' crops through till March and will stand a lot of frost.

Sowing Sow about ½ inch (1 cm) deep in a nursery bed, and thin to a plant every 3½ inches (8 cm).

Transplanting Seedlings should be 5 inches (12 cm) high before transplanting. Water well an hour before lifting, swirl the roots in a muddy puddle and plant 14 inches (35 cm) apart.

Cultivation Make sure that the planting bed is really firm, but if conditions are a bit wet, don't overdo it. Use the boot if wind or frost loosens the roots.

Fertiliser A handful of Growmore per sq yd (with bromophos) just before planting and a nitrogen fertiliser or foliar spray in late July or August.

Harvesting Always pick a few sprouts from each plant *from the bottom* of the stem. Most varieties will keep you going for 2 months.

SWEDES

Sow in June.

Soil Swede is not too fussy, but because it lasts right through to late spring, it will not tolerate bad drainage.

Position Some sun is essential and swedes do best in a very open position when the wind can keep the plants aired and healthy.

Varieties

Swedes are brassicas, subject to the diseases suffered by that family; 'Marian' is a good variety because it is resistant to clubroot and mildew. 'Purple Top' is an old trusty, and 'Best of All' is very hardy and will stand in the soil all winter. A delicious winter vegetable.

Sowing Sow thinly in a drill about ½ inch (1 cm) deep in the ground in which they will mature. Thin to 8 inches (20 cm).

Cultivation, Fertiliser and Harvesting Treat the soil with lime if necessary and firm the ground after raking in bromophos and Growmore. Dust against flea beetle at seedling stage or spray on sight of damage. Water in dry periods or the roots will go woody and split after rain.

Start eating some of the swedes as soon as they are big enough to make peeling worthwhile. The remainder will grow bigger when less crowded.

TURNIPS

Sow in March/April for earlies, or in August.
Soil Early crops need good soil and don't like sand. The winter varieties are more tolerant.
Position Some sun required.

Varieties

Early varieties come in three different shapes: flat, cylindrical and globe. 'Jersey Navet' is very early if sown under a cloche, as are 'Milan White Forcing' and 'Purple Top Milan'. However, if garden space is limited, there are tastier vegetables that merit preference. The same cannot be said of maincrop turnips: 'Golden Ball', sown in early August, and 'Manchester Market' are both good. Except in cold, wet land they will stand the winter, and earn a place as a delicious winter vegetable.
Sowing Sow ½ inch (1 cm) deep and thin early-sown seedlings to 5 inches (12 cm), maincrop to 10 inches (25 cm).
Cultivation If sowing maincrop turnips after an early vegetable, make sure that the soil is firm and lime if necessary. Dust the seedlings against flea beetle. Keep the soil moist at all times or turnips become woody and crack.
Fertiliser Rake in Growmore and bromophos before planting. A handful per sq yd will do.

♦ MISCELLANEOUS VEGETABLES ♦

GLOBE ARTICHOKES

Sow in April for a crop the following year, or buy or beg offsets.
Soil The globe artichoke does not like heavy clay soil, but you can, by incorporating a lot of compost, grow it in most soils.
Position In small gardens, dotted round the sunnier flower borders is the place for globe artichokes. A group in the vegetable patch takes up a lot of room, the plants are perennial and yield very little per sq yd. They like a bit of shelter.

Varieties

'Green Globe' is the one to grow from seed. Sow ¾ inch (2 cm) deep in a nursery bed, or better still in pots in a cold-frame. Slugs love the seedlings.

You may be lucky and find offsets on sale in a nursery or garden centre; or, best of all, beg one from a strong-growing plant in a neighbour's garden. They should be 8 inches (20 cm) high with a good root system (*right*).

Transplanting Transplant young plants into the vegetable garden at least 16 inches (40 cm) apart, or into the flower border wherever this yard-high, silvery, statuesque plant will look good.

Cultivation Prepare the ground as if you were planting a herbaceous clump or a small shrub – that is, dig in compost or peat. Keep well watered, and mulch round the stem to keep moist. Liquid feeding is desirable as the plants have to make a lot of growth prior to producing the globes.

Before the first frost, cut back to ground level and cover with straw or steaming compost to protect the roots from the cold.

Fertiliser Add a sprinkling of Growmore during the preparation of the planting bed, and give a liquid feed during the growing phase.

Difficulties Slugs are the main enemy. Aphids too can be a problem: spray as soon as you see them on the plants, remembering that they tend to go for the globes. Brown spots spreading on the flower head are a rare form of blight: cut off and burn. Your editor's plants seem to attract ants' nests round their roots. Apply pyrethrum if this happens to yours or you'll get weedy specimens and no globes.

Harvesting Do not wait until the scales on the globe begin to open, but cut when the head is still compact. Leave a few to flower: they are very handsome.

ASPARAGUS

Asparagus is one of life's little luxuries – and you *can* grow it successfully if you take the trouble. It can be grown from seed, but it is better to buy crowns unless you don't mind waiting several years for your first crop.

Soil As your editor has discovered to his cost, the absolute requirement is good drainage, but that can be arranged in any soil, and if you are keen enough, any soil can be coaxed into growing successful asparagus.

Position Shelter is important, and a not-too-shady spot.

Varieties

'Connover's Colossal' is a trusty variety that has been around for a long time. 'Suttons Perfection' is in the same category. Try ten crowns of one or the other for starters, then extend the bed with 'Lucullus' and 'Franklin' at either end.

Planting You can get seed, but treat yourself to crowns, one-year-olds are best. There are three years to wait between sowing seed and eating the shoots. Modern varieties of crowns promise a taste in a year. In heavyish soil the crowns need to be planted at or above the level of the rest of the garden, so you need to create a mound. The seedsman will deliver in March–April; don't let the crowns dry out, get them in and covered with about 4 inches (10 cm) of soil immediately. As the shoots or spears grow, keep covering them a little at a time until the soil is level with the top of the mound. *Don't* eat more than one spear.

Cultivation and Fertiliser Initially it really pays to do the job properly – after all, the plants are going to hog that bit of ground for ten, fifteen or even twenty years if you get it right. Autumn digging, incorporating lots of well-rotted organic matter is vital. If your soil is heavyish, leave it lumpy as you build your mound, and spread the compost or manure throughout. The frost and then worms will break down the clods.

In heavy soil you should plant asparagus crowns just above ground level, so your mound needs to be at least 10–12 inches (25–30 cm) high. Remember when digging that it will settle, so even 20 inches (50 cm) is not too high. Add a little bit of lime if the soil is very acid.

Get rid of every little root and top of every weed you see during digging. In March, as you await the crowns, dig over the mound again, breaking up any clods that remain. Add a sprinkling of Growmore at the same time.

As the spears turn into feathery stems, put in canes (taking care not to pierce the crowns) to support them. If they rock in the wind, the roots will be disturbed. When the leafy stems turn yellow in autumn, cut them back to 2 inches (5 cm) above mound level. Never be tempted to win favour with a friend by supplying the leafy ferns as floral tributes to his or her daughter finally getting her man to the altar: they are building up your personal treat for next spring!

In dry weather make sure that you keep the plants well watered, and weed by hand as accidents with a hoe can be disastrous. Mulch with a thin layer of compost.

In the March after planting, sprinkle more Growmore on the soil's surface, and as the spears appear, eat one from each plant – no more – just to prove to yourself that the trouble is worth while. Next year you can indulge yourself. Mulching and a little bit of Growmore will keep the plants going year after year, but watch the soil acidity and add lime if it rises. Stop cutting in mid-June to let the fronds grow to build up the plant for next year.

Difficulties There is an asparagus beetle (black with orange markings) which will eat stems, as will its grubs. Spray with liquid derris on sight. A purple mould and a reddish rust can infect plants – remove and burn at the first signs. Slugs can be a problem (see page 34). Any other problem is likely to be self-inflicted: frost damage due to failure to cover with a sack to prevent frost; loose roots resulting from unsupported ferns waving in the wind: and thin little spears caused by overcutting.

COURGETTES AND MARROWS

Sow in late May in the ground, or in pots on the windowsill in early May.
Soil The soil must be well prepared as for planting a shrub. Plenty of well-rotted compost and/or manure should be dug in, preferably in autumn. The plants must have reasonable drainage.
Position Sunny. Three or four plants are enough for most families. This is another vegetable that can be grown in the flower border if there is enough space (allow 1 sq yd per plant).

Varieties
'Long Green Bush' is a favourite. Pick young fruits as courgettes and let a few grow on to marrow size. 'Ambassador' is excellent and high-yielding. 'Zucchini' is very popular and early. 'Zebra Cross' is earlier than 'Long Green Bush' and high-yielding. 'Golden Zucchini' is an attractive variety for the flower border.

'Vegetable Spaghetti' is strictly a squash. It can be eaten fresh or will store in a frost-free shed or under the spare-room bed. 'Custard Marrows' grow convoluted and flattish and are very decorative; don't eat the seeds.

'Atlantic Giant' is *the* pumpkin. Redmond recommends it – but only grow one giant pumpkin per plant.
Sowing and Planting Sow in the ground in late May. Set two seeds together about ¾ inch (2 cm) deep and cover with cut-off plastic lemonade bottles. Pull out the weaker seedlings. Keep under a cover whenever there is any risk of frost.
Cultivation and Fertiliser Prepare the soil well, and include a handful of Growmore per sq yd.

If it's inclined to waterlogging, planting the young plants on a little mound will help drainage. Keep moist and mulch during growing. When the plants are fruiting, plenty of water with some tomato fertiliser added every 10 days or so will keep them in production. But don't overdo the water and put it around the roots not over the plant.
Difficulties Slugs are a pest at all stages (see page 34). Mildews and rots may be controlled by spray with carbendazim, but if the infections are bad, burn the offending bits or, better still, the whole plant. Fortunately, they are not very common and careful watering will deter them.

OUTDOOR TOMATOES

Sow indoors in April, or buy plants to put outdoors in June.

Soil Tomatoes need good soil, with well-rotted compost or manure dug in in autumn. Or grow outside in growbags or 9 inch (22.5 cm) pots.

Position Very sunny if you want the tomatoes to ripen. Another advantage of growbags or pots is that you can place them where you want – preferably against a south-facing wall or fence.

Varieties

Bush types are best: they don't require support or side shoot removal. 'Red Alert' is a favourite, with small, early fruit. 'Sub Arctic Plenty' is a good variety for the north. 'Tornado' bears a larger fruit with, it is claimed, a good flavour. 'The Amateur' is a heavy cropper, but perhaps not so tasty.

Cordon varieties need a stake and side shoots must be removed (*right*). 'Gardener's Delight' produces heavy crops of small, sweet-tasting tomatoes. 'Sweet 100' is even smaller, each fruit providing hardly a mouthful but there are plenty of them. 'Alicante', 'Ailsa Craig' and many of the others grown under glass can also be very successful outdoors, given the right conditions.

Sowing Sow in trays if you want a lot of plants. Sow thinly with just a covering of fine compost on top. Prick out into 3 inch (7.5 cm) pots at the two-leaf stage. Otherwise sow two seeds directly into the 3 inch (7.5 cm) pot and remove the weaker seedling.

Planting Out Plant out in June, in rows 18 inches (45 cm) apart, with 28 inches (70 cm) between rows.

Cultivation and Fertiliser The soil needs to be well dug and well-rotted compost worked in. Rake in Growmore and bromophos before planting. Cordon varieties should be staked at planting and tied at 8 inch (20 cm) intervals as they grow.

Watering is vital and something of an art, especially for tomatoes in growbags. Keep the soil or compost moist.

Feed with a tomato fertiliser according to the instructions on the bottle.

With bush varieties prevent the fruit from touching the soil by laying down straw or polythene.

Difficulties Tomatoes are subject to far too many problems, and the comfort in growing them outdoors is that there they should be slightly less vulnerable to some of them. Soil pests, aphids, rots, wilt and blight may cause damage. Cross your fingers, water carefully and don't splash the fruit, feed regularly and you'll probably grow a perfect, clean crop. If you have ripening problems, learn to make chutney.

> *REDMOND RECOMMENDS* **For the shy who find that tender loving embraces are few and far between, Titch has a simple remedy. 'My father had mistletoe growing on every apple tree in the garden. He cut an inch (2.5 cm) slit in the bark, eased it back and rubbed in a couple of berries, then pushed the bark back in place.' Apparently the mistletoe nearly always sprouted and grew, and for an improved love life it's a winner, if only during the festive season.**

◆ PRINCIPAL SEEDSMEN ◆

You can, of course, go round to your local shop and buy seeds, but it is unlikely to carry a very large selection, so it's worth sending off for seed catalogues and spending the winter perusing and planning. Catalogues are available from:

Boyce, J. W.
237 Carter Street,
Fordham,
Cambridgeshire
CB7 5JU.

Brown, D. T. & Co.
Ltd,
Station Road,
Poulton-le-Fylde,
Blackpool, FY7 HX.
(Tel. 0253 882371)

Butcher, Thomas
60 Wickham Road,
Shirley,
Croydon CR9 8AL.
(Tel. 01-655 0984)

Chiltern Seeds,
Bortree,
Stile,
Ulverston,
Cumbria LA12 7PB.

Samuel Dobie & Sons
Ltd,
Broomhill Way,
Torquay,
Devon TQ2 7QW.
(Tel. 0803 616281)

Marshall, S. E. & Co.
Ltd,
Regal Road,
Wisbech,
Cambridgeshire
PE13 2RF.
(Tel. 0945 583407)

Mr Fothergill's Seeds
Ltd,
Gazeley Road,
Kentford,
Newmarket,
Suffolk CB8 7QB.
(Tel. 0638 751887)

Suttons Seeds Ltd,
Hele Road,
Torquay,
Devon TQ2 7QJ.
(Tel. 0803 62011)

Thompson & Morgan
(Ipswich) Ltd,
London Road,
Ipswich,
Suffolk IP2 0BA.
(Tel. 0473 688588)

Unwins Seeds Ltd,
Histon,
Cambridgeshire
CB4 4LE.
(Tel. 022 023 588522)

◆ NURSERIES ◆

ENGLAND

Avon

Allen, I., & Huish, J.,
Belmont House,
Tyntesfield,
Wraxhall,
Bristol BS19 1NR.
(Tel. 027 583 2756)
*National Reference
Collection of asters*

Arne Herbs,
Limeburn Nurseries,
Limeburn Hill,
Chew Magna,
Avon BS18 8QW.
(Tel. 0272 333399)
Herbs

Blackmore and
Langdon Ltd,
Stanton Nurseries,
Pensford,
Bristol BS18 4JL.
*Begonias and
delphiniums*

Blagdon Water
Garden Centre Ltd,
Bath Road,
Upper Langford,
Avon BS18 7DN.
(Tel. 0934 852973)
Aquatic plants

Brackenwood
Nurseries,
131 Nore Road,
Portishead,
Nr Bristol,
Avon BS20 8DU.
(Tel. 0272 843484)
*Trees, shrubs, conifers
and alpines, many
unusual*

Glen Haven Gardens,
21 Dark Lane,
Blackwell,
Bristol BS19 3NT.
(Tel. 027 583 2700)
*General herbaceous
plants*

Lockyer, C. S.,
Lansbury,
70 Henfield Road,
Coalpit Heath,
Bristol BS17 2UZ.
(Tel. 0454 772219)
Fuchsias

Park Garden
Nurseries,
Over Lane,
Almondsbury,
Nr Bristol BS12 4BP.
(Tel. 0454 612247)
Herbaceous perennials

Berkshire

Carlile's Hardy Plants,
Twyford,
Reading,
Berkshire RG10 9PU.
Herbaceous plants

Crown Estate
Commissioners,
Savill Gardens,
The Great Park,
Windsor,
Berkshire SL4 2HT.
(Tel. 0753 860222)
*Mainly wholesale, but
exceptionally wide range
of choice trees, shrubs
and hardy plants*

Hollington Nurseries,
Woolton Hill,
Newbury,
Berkshire RG15 9XT.
(Tel. 0635 253908)
*Herbs, thymes, old-
fashioned roses and salvias;
cool conservatory plants*

Sherrards Garden
Centre Ltd,
Wantage Road,
Donnington,
Newbury,
Berkshire RG16 9BE.
*Trees, shrubs, conifers
and hardy plants*

Thames Valley Orchid
Society,
c/o 15 Weald Rise,
Tilehurst,
Reading,
Berkshire RG3 6XB.
Orchids

Thorp's Nurseries,
257 Finchampstead Road,
Wokingham,
Berkshire RG11 3JT.
*Regal and zonal
pelargoniums*

Wyld Court Orchids,
Hampstead Norreys,
Newbury,
Berkshire RG1 6BT.
Orchids

Buckinghamshire
Brackley, S. and N.,
117 Winslow Road,
Wingrave,
Aylesbury,
Buckinghamshire
HP22 4QB.
Sweet peas

Buckingham Nurseries,
Tingewick Road,
Buckingham
MK18 4AE.
(Tel. 0280 813556)
*Bare-rooted and
container-grown
hedging; trees and shrubs*

Butterfields Nursery,
Harvest Hill,
Bourne End,
Buckinghamshire
SL8 5JJ.
(Tel. 062 85 25455)
*Bare-rooted and
container-grown
hedging; trees and shrubs*

Morehavens,
28 Denham Lane,
Gerrards Cross,
Buckinghamshire
SL9 0EX.
(Tel. 024 07 3601)
Chamomiles

Wilton Park Nursery,
Park Lane,
Old Beaconsfield,
Buckinghamshire
HP9 2HT.
(Tel. 049 46 3418)
Small general nursery

Cambridgeshire
Honeysome Aquatic
Nursery,
The Row,
Sutton,
Nr Ely,
Cambridgeshire
CB6 2PF.
(Tel. 0353 778889)
*Hardy aquatic, bog and
marginal plants*

Ichiyo School of
Ikebana,
c/o Cherry Trees,
Providence Way,
Waterbeach,
Cambridgeshire
CB5 5QJ.
*Ikebana flower
arrangements*

Kerrielyn Fuchsias,
39 Holbrook Road,
Cambridge CB1 4SX.
Fuchsias

Marshall's Fen Bred
Seeds,
Regal Road,
Wisbech,
Cambridgeshire
PE13 2RF.
Vegetables

Oviatt-Ham, M.,
Ely House,
15 Green Street,
Willingham,
Cambridgeshire
CB4 5JA.
(Tel. 0945 60481)
*Clematis and climbing
plants*

Treatharp Ltd,
Elm House Nursery,
Walpole St Peter,
Wisbech,
Cambridgeshire
PE14 7PJ.
(Tel. 0945 780444)
*Chrysanthemums,
fuchsias, carnations,
geraniums*

Cheshire
Bridgemere Garden
World,
Bridgemere,
Nr Nantwich,
Cheshire CW5 7QB.
(Tel. 09365 381/3)
*National collections of
cimicifuga and kniphofia
plus very wide range of
crocosmia*

Caddick's Clematis,
Rushgreen Garden
Centre,
Dyer's Lane,
Rushgreen Road,
Lymm,
Cheshire WA13 9QL.
(Tel. 092 575 6606)
Clematis

Caldwell & Sons Ltd,
The Nurseries,
Chelford Road,
Knutsford,
Cheshire WA16 8LX.
(Tel. 0565 4281/2)
Wide general range

Collinwood Nurseries,
Mottram St Andrew,
Macclesfield,
Cheshire SK10 4QR.
Chrysanthemums

Fryers Nurseries Ltd,
Knutsford,
Cheshire.
Roses

Jackson, Joseph S. & Son,
Post Office Nurseries,
Kettleshulme,
Stockport,
Cheshire SJ12 7RD.
(Tel. 06633 2632)
Pansies, violas, violettas

Lismore Alpines,
Northwich Road,
Cranage,
Holmes Chapel,
Cheshire CW4 3HL.
(Tel. 0477 32699)
*Connoisseur alpines,
especially androsaces,
campanulas, dionysias,
primulas, saxifrages and
gentians*

Sealand Nurseries Ltd,
Sealand,
Chester CH1 6BA.
*Astilbes, peonies, lilies
and roses*

Stapeley Water
Gardens Ltd,
92 London Road,
Stapeley,
Nantwich,
Cheshire CW5 7LH.
(Tel. 0270 623868)
*Europe's largest water
garden; full range of
appropriate plants and
equipment*

Walker, Harold,
Oakfield Nurseries,
Huntington,
Chester CH3 6EA.
(Tel. 0244 20731)
*Chrysanthemums and
spring bedding plants*

Ward Fuchsias,
5 Pollen Close,
Sale,
Cheshire M33 3LP.
(Tel. 061 973 6467)
Fuchsias

Cornwall

Bosvigo Plants,
Bosvigo House,
Bosvigo Lane,
Truro,
Cornwall TR1 3NH.
(Tel. 0872 75774)
*Unusual herbaceous
plants*

Bregover Plants,
Hillbrooke,
Middlewood,
North Hill,
Launceston,
Cornwall PL15 7NN.
(Tel. 0566 82661)
*Primulas and border
plants for damp and
shade; also auriculas,
violets and geraniums*

Burncoose and
Southdown Nurseries,
Gwennap,
Redruth,
Cornwall TR16 6BJ.
(Tel. 0209 861112)
*Trees, shrubs and
ornamental plants*

Duchy of Cornwall
Woodlands,
Penlyne Nursery,
Cott Road,
Lostwithiel,
Cornwall PL22 0BW.
(Tel. 0208 872668)
General nursery

The Lanhydrock
Gardens (NT),
Lanhydrock,
Bodmin,
Cornwall PL30 5AD.
(Tel. 0208 2220)
*Shrubs, especially
camellias, azaleas,
rhododendrons,
magnolias, deutzias,
philadelphus and ceanothus*

Mallorn Gardens,
Lanner Hill,
Redruth,
Cornwall TR16 6DA.
(Tel. 0209 215931)
*Wide and often changing
general range*

Parkinson Herbs,
Barras Moor Farm,
Perran-ar-Worthal,
Truro,
Cornwall.
(Tel. 0872 864380)
Herbs

Polyphant Herb Garden,
Polyphant,
Launceston,
Cornwall PL15 7PS.
(Tel. 0566 86578)
Herbs

Porthpean House Gardens,
Porthpean,
St Austell,
Cornwall.
(Tel. 0726 72888)
*Camellias and shrubs for
acid soils*

Roskellan Nursery,
Maenlay, Helston,
Cornwall TR12 7QR.
(Tel. 0326 572657)
*Shrubs, climbers and
herbs; rooted cuttings*

Tomperrow Farm
Nurseries,
Tomperrow Farm,
Threemilestone,
Truro,
Cornwall TR3 6BE.
(Tel. 0872 560344)
Herbaceous perennials

Trewithen Nurseries,
Grampound Road,
Truro,
Cornwall TR2 4DD.
(Tel. 0726 882764)
*Shrubs, especially
camellias and
rhododendrons*

Wall Cottage Nursery,
Lockengate,
Bugle,
St Austell,
Cornwall PL28 8RU.
(Tel. 0208 831259)
*Rhododendrons and
azaleas plus general range*

Warrick, M.,
Lower Trenode,
Widegates,
Looe,
Cornwall.
(Tel. 050 34 270)
Chamomiles

Cumbria
Currie, Fred (Dahlias),
20 Rydal Mount,
Kendal,
Cumbria LA9 4RS.
(Tel. 0539 25410)
Dahlias

Hartside Nursery Garden,
Low Gill House,
Alston,
Cumbria CA9 3BL.
(Tel. 0498 81372)
*Alpines grown at
1100 ft (335 m) in
Pennines*

Hayes Garden World,
Lake District
Nurseries,
Ambleside,
Cumbria LA22 0DW.
(Tel. 053 94 33434)
Perennials

Larch Cottage
Nurseries,
Melkinthorpe,
Penrith,
Cumbria CA10 2DR.
(Tel. 093 12 404)
Unusual plants

Weasdale Nurseries,
Newbiggin-on-Lune,
Kirkby Stephen,
Cumbria CA17 4LX.
(Tel. 058 73 246)
*Hardy forest trees,
hedging and ornamental
shrubs grown at 850 ft
(260 m) above sea level*

Yates, Geoffrey,
Stagshaw,
Ambleside,
Cumbria LA22 0HE.
(Tel. 0966 32109)
*Heathers,
rhododendrons, azaleas,
shrubs, ground-cover
and woodland plants*

Derbyshire
Bebbington, Tom,
Dahlias,
Lady Gate Nursery,
47 The Green,
Diseworth,
Derbyshire DE7 2QN.
(Tel. 0332 811565)
*Dahlias and exhibition
begonias*

Ednaston Manor
Gardens Ltd,
Brailsford,
Derby DE6 3BA.
(Tel. 0335 60325)
*Wide range of
herbaceous plants,
shrubs, alpines and old
roses*

Highgates Nursery,
166a Crich Lane,
Belper,
Derbyshire DE5 1EP.
(Tel. 077 382 2153)
Alpines

Rileys
Chrysanthemums,
Alfreton Nurseries,
Woolley Moor,
Derby DE5 6FF.
Chrysanthemums

Devon
Bowden, Anne &
Roger,
Cleave House,
Sticklepath,
Okehampton,
Devon EX20 2NN.
(Tel. 0837 84 0481)
Hostas

Burnham Nurseries
Ltd,
Forches Cross,
Newton Abbott,
Devon TQ12 6PZ.
Orchids

Churchills Garden
Nursery,
Exeter Road,
Chudleigh,
South Devon
TQ13 0DD.
(Tel. 0626 852585)
*Small general range of
plants, many unusual*

The Fortescue Garden Trust,
The Garden House,
Buckland Monachorum,
Yelverton,
Devon PL20 7LQ.
(Tel. 0822 854769)
General herbaceous plants, trees and shrubs

The High Garden,
Courtwood,
Newton Ferrers,
South Devon EX38 7EG.
Pieris and rhododendrons

Kenwith Castle Nurseries Ltd,
Bideford,
North Devon EX39 5BE.
(Tel. 02372 3712)
All conifer genera; grafting a speciality; many new introductions to UK

Knightshayes Garden Trust,
The Garden Office,
Knightshayes,
Tiverton,
Devon EX16 7RG.
(Tel. 0884 253264)
Shrubs and herbaceous plants; plant list available at the Plant Centre

Marwood Hill Gardens,
Barnstaple,
North Devon
EX31 4EB.
(Tel. 0271 42528)
Large range of unusual trees and shrubs; eucalyptus, alpines, camellias and bog plants

Otter Nurseries Ltd,
Gosford Road,
Ottery St Mary,
Devon EX11 1LZ.
(Tel. 040 481 3341/2)
Small general nursery.

Perrie Hale Nursery,
Northcote Hill,
Honiton,
Devon EX14 8TH.
(Tel. 0404 3344)
Trees, hedging plants and shrubs

Peveril Clematis Nursery,
Christow,
Exeter,
Devon EX6 7NG.
(Tel. 0647 52937)
Clematis

Rosemoor Garden Trust,
Torrington,
Devon EX2 7JY.
(Tel. 0805 24067)
National cornus collection; ilex and rare plants and shrubs

St Bridget Nurseries Ltd,
Old Rydon Lane,
Exeter,
Devon EX2 7JY.
(Tel. 0392 87 3672/3/4)
Large general nursery

Southcombe Garden Plant Nursery,
Widecombe-in-the-Moor,
Newton Abbott,
Devon TQ13 7TU.
(Tel. 036 42 214)
General nursery

Stone Lane Gardens,
Stone Farm,
Chagford,
Devon TQ13 8JU.
(Tel. 0647 23311)
Wide range of wild provenance betula and alnus

Torbay's Plant World,
St Marychurch Road,
Newton Abbott,
Devon.
(Tel. 0803 872939)
Alpines

Wills, H. & J.,
2 St Brannocks Park Road,
Ilfracombe,
Devon EX34 8HU.
(Tel. 0271 63949)
Sempervivums

Yearlstone Vineyard,
Chilton,
Bickleigh,
Tiverton,
Devon EX16 8RT.
(Tel. 088 45 450)
Vines

Dorset
Fairview Nursery,
Newmans Lane,
Westmoors,
Dorset BH22 0LW.
(Tel. 0202 877745)
Rare and unusual perennials

C. W. Groves & Son,
West Bay Road,
Bridport,
Dorset DT6 4BA.
(Tel. 0308 22654)
Garden centre specialising in Parma and hardy violas.

John of Dorset,
Avonmoor,
Matchams Lane,
Hurn,
Christchurch,
Dorset BH23 6AA.
(Tel. 0202 517139)
Heathers

The Knoll Gardens,
Stapehill Road,
Stapehill,
Wimborne,
Dorset BH21 7ND.
(Tel. 0202 873931)
*General, particularly
herbaceous plants; range
alters considerably each
year*

Macpennys,
15 Bransgore,
Christchurch,
Dorset BH23 8DB.
(Tel. 0425 72348)
General nursery

Naked Cross Nurseries,
Waterloo Road,
Corfe Mullen,
Wimborne,
Dorset BH21 3SR.
(Tel. 0202 693256)
*Heathers and herbaceous
plants*

Rivendell Alpines,
Horton Heath,
Wimborne,
Dorset BH21 7JN.
(Tel. 0202 824013)
Alpines

Three Counties
Nurseries,
Marshwood,
Bridport,
Dorset DT6 5QJ,
(Tel. 029 77 257)
Pinks and dianthus

Trehane Camellia
Nursery,
J. Trehane & Sons Ltd,
Staplehill Road,
Hampreston,
Wimborne,
Dorset BH21 7NE.
(Tel. 0202 873490)
Hardy camellias

Durham
Rookhope Nurseries,
Rookhope,
Upper Weardale,
County Durham
DL13 2DD.
(Tel. 0388 517272)
*Truly hardy plants for
exposed and difficult
conditions*

East Sussex
A.P. Elite Plants,
A.P. Nursery,
Vines Cross,
Heathfield,
East Sussex.
*Peltatum and zonal
pelargoniums*

Axletree Nursery,
Starvecrow Lane,
Peasmarsh,
Rye,
East Sussex TN31 6XL.
(Tel. 079 721 470)
*Small general range,
especially geraniums and
euphorbias*

Fairlight Camellia
Nursery,
Three Oaks Village,
Guestling,
Nr Hastings,
East Sussex.
(Tel. 0424 425371)
*Old rare and modern
hybrid camellias*

Funnell's Farm
Nurseries,
Maynards Green,
Heathfield,
East Sussex TN21 0DB.
(Tel. 043 53 2367)
*130 varieties of clematis
plus other climbers,
alpines, geraniums,
fuchsias*

Great Dixter
Nurseries,
Northiam,
Rye,
East Sussex TN31 6PH.
(Tel. 079 74 3107)
*Clematis, shrubs and
plants; gardens open*

Long Man Garden,
Lewes Road,
Wilmington,
Polegate,
East Sussex BN26 5RS.
(Tel. 0323 870816)
*Mainly conservatory
plants; some hardy
climbers; conifers and
hardy perennials*

McBeans Orchids Ltd,
Cooksbridge,
Lewes,
Sussex.
Orchids

Nielsen Plants Ltd,
Danecroft Nurseries,
Station Road,
Hellingly,
East Sussex BN27 4EU.
*Begonias, hibiscus,
campanulas,
pelargoniums and
miniature roses*

Oakdene Nursery,
Scotsford Road,
Broad Oak,
Heathfield,
East Sussex
TN21 8TU.
(Tel. 043 52 4382)
Alpines, bulbs and
shrubs

Perryhill Nurseries,
Hartfield,
East Sussex TN7 4JP.
(Tel. 089 277 377)
Over 750 herbaceous
and 270 shrub and
climbing roses; trees,
shrubs, conifers and
rhododendrons

Sifelle Nursery,
The Walled Garden,
Newick Park,
Newick,
East Sussex.
(Tel. 082 572 3073)
General; scented and
aromatic plants and
salvias

Sussex Country
Gardens,
Newhaven Road,
Kingston,
Nr Lewes,
East Sussex BN7 3NE.
(Tel. 0273 473510)
Hostas and geraniums

Essex
Baker, B. & H. M.,
Bourne Brook
Nurseries,
Greenstead Green,
Halstead,
Essex CO9 1RJ.
(Tel. 0787 472900/
476369)
Fuchsias

Bourne Bridge
Nurseries,
Oak Hill Road,
Stapleford Abbotts,
Romford,
Essex RM4 1JL.
Bonsai

British Bedding Plant
Association,
Agriculture House,
New London Road,
Chelmsford,
Essex CM2 0AP.
Annuals grown from
seed.

Bullwood Nursery,
54 Woodlands Road,
Hockley,
Essex SS5 4PY.
(Tel. 0702 203761)
Mainly Liliaceae; also a
wide range of shrubs,
some uncommon and
rare

Cants of Colchester
Ltd,
Agriculture House,
305 Mile End Road,
Colchester,
Essex CO4 5EB.
Roses

Carnivorous Plant
Society,
c/o 24 Osborne Road,
Brentwood,
Essex CM15 9LE.
Carnivorous plants

Chatto, Beth,
Gardens,
Elmstead Market,
Colchester,
Essex CO7 7DB.
Hardy herbaceous
perennial plants for dry
and damp conditions

Cottage Gardens,
Langham Road,
Boxted,
Colchester,
Essex CO4 5HU.
(Tel. 0206 272269)
General nursery

County Park Nursery,
Essex Gardens,
Hornchurh,
Essex RM11 3BU.
(Tel. 040 24 45205)
Alpines and rare and
unusual plants from
New Zealand,
Tasmania and Falklands

Frye, M. G.,
The Willows,
Poors Lane North,
Daws Heath,
Thundersley,
Essex SS7 2XF.
(Tel. 0702 558467)
Heathers

Hull Farm,
Spring Valley Lane,
Ardleigh,
Colchester,
Essex CO7 7SB.
(Tel. 0206 230045)
Conifers

Langthorns Plantery,
High Cross Lane West,
Little Canfield,
Dunmow,
Essex CM6 1TD.
(Tel. 0371 2611)
Wide general range with
many unusual plants

M. & R. Plants,
73 Cecil Avenue,
Hornchurch,
Essex RM11 2NA.
Alpines and hardy
perennials

Mansfield Nurseries,
Eastwood Rise,
Eastwood,
Essex SS9 5DA.
(Tel. 0702 525410)
*Alpines, heathers and
dwarf conifers*

Muir, Ken,
Honeypot Farm,
Rectory Road,
Weeley Heath,
Clacton-on-Sea,
Essex CO16 9BJ.
Berried fruits

Potash Nursery,
Hawkwell,
Hockley,
Essex SS5 4JY.
Fuchsias

Ramparts Nurseries,
Bakers Lane,
Braiswick,
Colchester,
Essex CO4 5BB.
*Pinks and grey foliage
plants*

Whitehouse Ivies,
Hylands Farm,
Rectory Road,
Tolleshunt Knights,
Essex CM9 8EZ.
(Tel. 0621 815782)
*Over 300 varieties of
hedera*

Gloucestershire
Highfield Nurseries,
Whitminster,
Gloucester GL2 7PL.
*Conifers, ferns, fruit
trees, herbaceous plants,
herbs, roses and shrubs*

Lechlade Garden &
Fuchsia Centre,
Fairford Road,
Lechlade,
Gloucestershire
GL7 3DP.
(Tel. 0367 52372)
*Over 500 varieties of
fuchsia*

Mount Pleasant Trees,
Rockhampton,
Berkeley,
Gloucestershire
GL13 9DU.
(Tel. 0454 260348)
*Common and rare
shrubs for hedging,
arboreta, forestry and
gardens*

Old Manor Nursery,
Twyning,
Gloucestershire
GL20 6DB.
(Tel. 0684 293516)
*Predominantly alpines;
but with small supply of
unusual and rare
varieties*

Osmond, George,
Archfield Nursery,
Wickwar,
Wotton-under-Edge,
Gloucestershire
GL12 8NA.
(Tel. 045 424 216)
*Mainly alpines, ericaceous
plants and conifers*

Pattison, Chris,
Brookend,
Pendock,
Gloucestershire
GL19 3PL.
(Tel. 053 181 480)
*Choice and rare shrubs
and alpines*

The Priory,
Kemerton,
Tewkesbury,
Gloucestershire.
(Tel. 038 689 258)
General nursery

Thuya Alpine
Nursery,
Glebelands,
Hartpury,
Gloucestershire
GL19 3BW.
(Tel. 045 270 548)
*Wide and changing
range, including rarities*

Greater Manchester
All-In-One Garden
Centre,
Rochdale Road,
Middleton,
Manchester M24 2RB.
(Tel. 0706 32793)
Herbaceous plants

The Vicarage Garden,
Carrington,
Urmston,
Manchester
M31 4AG.
(Tel. 061 775 2750)
*Geraniums, campanulas
and dwarf varieties of
other perennials*

Hampshire
Anmore Tropical
Botanic Gardens Ltd,
Sir George Staunton
Estate,
Petersfield Road,
Havant,
Hampshire PO9 5HB.
Tropical plants

Bailey, Steven, Ltd,
Eden Nurseries,
Silver Street,
Sway,
Lymington,
Hampshire SO41 6ZA.
*Carnations, pinks,
gerberas, dwarf hardy
garden alstroemerias*

Everton Nurseries Ltd,
Everton,
Nr Lymington,
Hampshire SO4 0JZ.
(Tel. 0590 42155)
Wide general range

Exbury Gardens,
Exbury,
Nr Southampton,
Hampshire SO4 1AZ.
(Tel. 0703 891203)
*Rhododendrons, azaleas,
camellias*

Glenside Bonsai,
22 Water Lane,
Totton,
Southampton,
Hampshire SO4 3DP.
Bonsai

Hayward's Carnations,
The Chace Gardens,
Stakes Road,
Purbrook,
Portsmouth PO7 5PL.
(Tel. 0705 263047)
*Hardy pinks and border
carnations; greenhouse
perpetual carnations*

Higher End Nursery,
Hale,
Fordingbridge,
Hampshire SP6 2RA.
(Tel. 0725 22243)
*Water-lilies; bog and
marginal plants, especially
hellebores, rodgersias, trollius;
asters*

Hillier Nurseries
(Winchester) Ltd,
Ampfield House,
Ampfield,
Nr Romsey,
Hampshire SO51 9PA.
(Tel. 0794 68733)
*Very large range of trees,
shrubs, conifers,
climbers, roses, fruit and
hardy perennials*

House, Philip (Family
Trees),
Botley,
Hampshire SO3 2EA.
(Tel. 048 92 6680)
Ornamental trees

Longstock Park Nursery,
Stockbridge,
Hampshire SO20 6EH.
(Tel. 0264 810894)
*Shrubs and conifers;
water gardens and
aquatic plants*

Oakleigh Nurseries,
Monkwood,
Alresford,
Hampshire SO24 0HB.
(Tel. 0962 77344)
Fuchsias and pelargoniums

Orchardleigh Nursery,
Botley Road,
Bishop's Waltham,
Southampton,
Hampshire SO3 1DR.
(Tel. 048 93 2687)
Alpines and heathers

Southview Nurseries,
Chequers Lane,
Eversley Cross,
Basingstoke,
Hampshire RG27 0NT.
(Tel. 0734 732206)
*Cottage garden plants;
pinks and cowslips*

Spinners,
Boldre,
Lymington,
Hampshire
SO41 5QE.
(Tel. 0590 73347)
*Plants and shrubs for
shade; acers, magnolias,
hostas, geraniums and
daphnes*

Trenear, Peter,
Chantreyland,
Chequers Lane,
Eversley Cross,
Hampshire
RG27 0NX.
(Tel. 0734 732300)
*Geraniums, hebes,
helianthemums, hostas,
pulmonarias, vincas,
shrubs and conifers*

Hereford and Worcester

Abbey Dore Court
Gardens,
Abbeydore,
Hereford and
Worcester HR2 0AD.
(Tel. 0981 240419)
*Unusual shrubs,
herbaceous plants and
alpines; NCCPG
collection of sedums and
euphorbias*

Ballard, Helen,
Old Country,
Mathon,
Malvern,
Hereford and
Worcester WR13 5PS.
(Tel. 0886 880 215)
*Snowdrops and
hellebores, mainly hybrid
orientalis*

R. F. Beeston,
Owen Bros Nursery,
294 Ombersley Road,
Worcester WR3 7HD.
(Tel. 0905 53245)
*New and rare alpines,
especially from Turkey,
Kashmir and Nepal*

Bouts Cottage
Nurseries,
Bouts Lane,
Nr Inkberrow,
Hereford and
Worcester.
Violas and pansies

Cooper, Mrs Susan,
Churchfields House,
Cradley,
Malvern,
Hereford and
Worcester WR13 5LJ
(Tel. 0886 880 223)
*Rare and unusual trees
and shrubs*

The Cottage Herbery,
Mill House,
Boraston,
Nr Tenbury Wells,
Hereford and
Worcester WR15 8LZ.
(Tel. 058 479 575)
*Over 200 varieties of
herbs*

Eastgrove Cottage
Garden Nursery,
Sankyns Green,
Little Witley,
Nr Shrawley,
Hereford and
Worcester WR6 6LQ.
(Tel. 0299 896389)
*Hardy plants, especially
for the 'old world
country flower garden'*

Fuchsiavale Nurseries,
Stanklyn Lane,
Summerfield,
Kidderminster,
Hereford and
Worcester DY10 4HS.
(Tel. 0562 69444)
Fuchsias

Greenacres Nursery,
Bringsty Common,
Bromyard,
Hereford and
Worcester WR6 5TA.
(Tel. 0885 82206)
Heathers

Kingstone Cottage Plants,
West-under-Penyar,
Ross-on-Wye,
Hereford HR9 7NXL.
(Tel. 0989 65267)
Dianthus

Old Court Nurseries Ltd,
Colwell,
Nr Malvern,
Hereford and
Worcester WR13 6QE.
(Tel. 0684 40416)
*General; home of
Ballard Michaelmas
daisies*

Rushfields of Ledbury,
Ross Road,
Ledbury,
Hereford and
Worcester HR8 2LP.
(Tel. 0531 2004)
*Unusual herbaceous and
foliage plants*

Stoke Lacy Herb Garden,
Bromyard,
Hereford and
Worcester HR4 7JH.
(Tel. 0432 820232)
Herbs

Stone House Cottage
Nurseries,
Stone,
Nr Kidderminster,
Hereford and
Worcester.
(Tel. 0562 69902)
*Small general range,
especially wall shrubs;
climbers and unusual
plants*

Treasures of Tenbury Ltd,
Burford House
Gardens,
Tenbury Wells,
Hereford and
Worcester WR15 8HQ.
(Tel. 0584 810777)
*Clematis and wide
general range, including
many unusual plants*

Wintergreen
Nurseries,
Bringsty Common,
Hereford and
Worcester WR6 5UW.
(Tel. 0886 21835)
*General, especially
alpines*

Hertfordshire
Blom, Walter, and
Son Ltd,
Coombelands Nurseries,
Leavesden,
Watford,
Hertfordshire WD2 7BH.
Tulips

Growing Carpets,
The Old Farmhouse,
Steeple Morden,
Hertfordshire SG8 0PP.
(Tel. 0763 852417)
*Wide range of ground-
cover plants*

Harkness, R. & Co. Ltd,
The Rose Garden,
Hitchin,
Hertfordshire.
Roses

Harveys Garden
Centre,
Bragbury Lane,
Stevenage,
Hertfordshire SG2 8TJ.
(Tel. 0438 811777)
Herbaceous plants

Hatfield House Garden
Shop,
Hatfield House,
Hertfordshire AL9 5NQ.
(Tel. 070 72 64412
ext. 245)
*Old-fashioned roses and
shrubs*

Hopleys Plants Ltd,
Much Hadham,
Hertfordshire
SG10 6BU.
*Hardy and half-hardy
perennials*

Maydencroft Aquatic
Nurseries,
Maydencroft Lane,
Gosmore,
Hitchin,
Hertfordshire SG4 7QD.
(Tel. 0462 56020)
*Water-lilies, marginal
and bog plants, alpines,
dwarf conifers*

Priorswood Clematis,
Priorswood,
Widbury Hill,
Ware,
Hertfordshire
SG12 7QH.
(Tel. 0920 61543)
Clematis

Tokonoma Bonsai Ltd,
14 London Road,
Shenley,
Radlett,
Hertfordshire WD7 9EN.
Bonsai

Humberside
Marston, J. & D.,
Culag,
Green Lane,
Nafferton,
Great Driffield,
Humberside YO25 8SU.
(Tel. 0377 44487)
*Hardy and greenhouse
ferns*

Southfield Nurseries,
Louth Road,
Holton-le-Clay,
Grimsby,
South Humberside
DN36 5HL.
Cacti and succulents

Isle of Man
Ballalheannagh Gardens,
Glen Roy,
Lonan,
Isle of Man.
(Tel. 0624 781875)
General nursery

Isle of Wight
Cranmore Vine Nursery,
Yarmouth,
Isle of Wight
PO41 0XY.
(Tel. 0983 760080)
Grape vines

Kent
Bamboo Nursery,
Kinsgate Cottage,
Wittersham,
Tenterden,
Kent TN30 7NS.
(Tel. 07977 607)
Bamboo

Bradshaw, J., & Son,
Busheyfield Nursery,
Herne,
Herne Bay,
Kent CT6 7LJ.
(Tel. 0227 375415)
*Clematis and climbers
(mainly wholesale);
NCCPG collection of
climbing loniceras*

Cawthorne,
R. G. M.,
Lower Daltons
Nursery,
Swanley Village,
Swanley,
Kent BR8 7NU.
*Violas, violettas and
viola species*

Crown Point Nursery,
Ightham,
Nr Sevenoaks,
Kent TN15 0HB.
*Rhododendrons, azaleas,
shrubs, trees and
ground-cover plants*

Hazeldene Nursery,
Dean Street,
East Farleigh,
Maidstone,
Kent ME15 0PS.
Pansies and violas

Henderson, C. E., &
Son,
Leydens Nursery,
Stick Hill,
Edenbridge,
Kent TN8 5NH.
(Tel. 0732 863318)
*Hardy trees and shrubs,
roses, heathers, conifers;
wild British flowers,
cowslips, primulas*

Hever Castle Ltd,
Edenbridge,
Kent TN8 7NG.
Hydrangeas

Hyatt, B., Auriculas,
1 Toddington
Crescent,
Bluebell Hill,
Chatham,
Kent ME5 9QT.
(Tel. 0634 63251)
Auriculas

Iden Croft Herbs,
Frittenden Road,
Staplehurst,
Kent TN12 0DH.
*Edible flowers and herbs;
plants which attract
butterflies and bees;
alpine plants*

Ingram, Tim,
Copton Ash,
105 Ashford Road,
Faversham,
Kent ME13 8XW.
(Tel. 0795 535919)
Unusual plants

Oldbury Nurseries,
Brissenden Green,
Bethersden,
Kent TN26 3BJ.
Fuchsias

Old Rectory Herb Garden,
Ightham,
Kent TN15 9AL.
(Tel. 0732 882608)
*Herbs and aromatic
plants*

Orchid Society of
Great Britain,
c/o 120 Grofton Road,
Orpington,
Kent BR6 2HZ.
Orchids

G. Reuthe Ltd,
Foxhill Nursery,
Jackass Lane,
Keston,
Nr Bromley,
Kent BR2 6AW.
(Tel. 0689 52249)
*Rhododendrons, azaleas,
trees, shrubs and conifers*

Robinsons Hardy
Plants,
Greencourt Nurseries,
Crockenhill,
Swanley,
Kent BR8 8HD.
*Dwarf and unusual
perennials*

Ruxley Manor Garden
Centre,
Maidstone Road,
Sidcup,
Kent DA14 5BQ.
(Tel. 01-300 0084)
Herbaceous plants

Smith, Alan C.,
127 Leaves Green Road,
Keston,
Kent BR2 6DG.
(Tel. 0959 72531)
*Over 1,000 sempervivums
and jovibarbas*

Starborough Nursery,
Starborough Road,
Marsh Green,
Edenbridge,
Kent TN8 5RB.
*Rare and unusual
shrubs, rhododendrons
and azaleas*

Wallace & Barr,
The Nurseries,
Marden,
Kent TN12 9BP.
(Tel. 0622 831235)
Wide general range

Washfield Nursery,
Hawkhurst,
Kent TN18 4QU.
(Tel. 05805 2522)
*Mainly small woodland
plants: hellebores,
epimediums, geraniums,
etc.*

The Weald Herbary,
Park Cottage,
Frittenden,
Cranbrook,
Kent TN17 2AU.
(Tel. 0580 80 226)
Herbs and aromatics

Wells & Winter,
Mere House,
Mereworth,
Maidstone,
Kent ME18 5NB.
*Herbs and variegated
plants; dwarf conifers
and alpines*

Lancashire
Barton Grange Garden
Centre,
Garstang Road,
Barton,
Preston,
Lancashire PR3 5AA.
(Tel. 0772 862551)
Herbaceous plants

Bents Garden Centre
and Nurseries,
Warrington Road,
Glazebury,
Nr Leigh,
Lancashire
WA3 5NT.
(Tel. 0942 671028)
*Wide range of astilbes,
hemerocallis, hellebores,
Japanese anemones and
meconopsis*

Deeside Gardens,
Norman Leisure Ltd,
37 Grains Road,
Shaw,
Oldham,
Lancashire OL2 8HZ.
(Tel. 0706 845418)
*Fuchsias and aquatic
plants*

Genus Primula,
Harbour House,
Glasson Dock,
Lancaster LA2 0BU.
(Tel. 0524 770357)
Primulas and acers

Holden Clough
Nursery,
Holden,
Bolton-by-Bowland,
Clitheroe,
Lancashire BB7 4PF.
(Tel. 020 07 615)
*Large general list
including primulas,
saxifrages, pulmonarias,
androsaces, astilbes,
gentians*

Kaye, Reginald, Ltd,
Waithman Nurseries,
Silverdale,
Carnforth,
Lancashire LA5 0TY.
(Tel. 0524 701252)
*Hardy ferns, alpines,
herbaceous plants, some
shrubs*

Pinks and Carnations,
22 Chetwyn Avenue,
Bromley Cross,
Bolton,
Lancashire BL7 9BN.
(Tel. 0204 56273)
*Pinks and perpetual
carnations*

Samlesbury Bonsai
Nursery,
Potters Lane,
Samlesbury,
Preston,
Lancashire PR5 0UE.
Bonsai

Stydd Nursery,
Stonygate Lane,
Ribchester,
Nr Preston,
Lancashire PR3 3YN.
*Roses; ornamental
foliage and herbaceous
plants*

Swallow Villas
Nurseries,
147 Liverpool Old
Road,
Much Hoole,
Nr Preston,
Lancashire PR4 4GB.
(Tel. 0772 613016)
*Foliage and unusual
perennials; hardy
geraniums, pulmonarias,
variegated plants and
grasses*

Tivey, Philip, & Son,
28 Wanlip Road,
Syston,
Lancashire LE7 8PA.
(Tel. 0533 692968)
Dahlias

Wingates,
62A Chorley Road,
Westhoughton,
Bolton,
Lancashire BL5 3PL.
(Tel. 0942 813357)
*Mainly heathers; also
dwarf conifers and
shrubs, ericaceous plants
and alpines.*

Leicestershire
Goscote Nurseries Ltd,
Syston Road,
Crossington,
Leicestershire LE7 8NZ.
(Tel. 050981 2121)
*Trees, shrubs, heathers,
conifers, alpines, herbaceous
plants; specialist in* Ericaceae

Kayes Garden Nursery,
1700 Melton Road,
Rearsby,
Leicester LE7 8YR.
(Tel. 066 474 578)
General nursery

Rearsby Roses Ltd,
Melton Road,
Rearsby,
Leicester LE7 8YP.
Roses

Smith, John, & Son Ltd,
Hilltop Nurseries,
Thornton,
Leicestershire LE6 1AN.
(Tel. 0530 230331)
*Hardy and half-hardy
fuchsias, dwarf conifers,
heathers, hardy plants
and shrubs*

Tivey, P., and Sons,
28 Wanlip Road,
Syston,
Nr Leicester.
*Chrysanthemums and
dahlias*

Wingwell Nursery,
Top Street,
Wing,
Oakham,
Leicestershire LE15 8SE.
(Tel. 057 285 400)
*Low-maintenance
herbaceous plants,
especially ground-cover
and small shrubs*

Lincolnshire
Candlesby Herbs,
Cross Keys Cottage,
Candlesby,
Spilsby,
Lincolnshire PE23 5SF.
(Tel. 075 485 211)
Herbs

Careby Manor Gardens,
Careby,
Stamford,
Lincolnshire PE9 4EA.
(Tel. 07808 1220)
*Rare and unusual
plants; plant list
available at garden*

Foliage and Unusual
Plants,
The Dingle,
Pilsgate,
Stamford,
Lincolnshire PE9 3HW.
(Tel. 0780 740775)
*Variegated, coloured-
leaved and unusual
plants*

Jefferson-Brown,
Michael, Ltd,
Broadgate,
Weston Hills,
Spalding,
Lincolnshire PE12 6DQ.
Daffodils

Martin Nest Nurseries,
Grange Cottage,
Harpswell Lane,
Hemswell,
Gainsborough,
Lincolnshire DN21 5UP.
(Tel. 042 773 369)
*Alpines, especially
auriculas, primulas,
androsaces, lewisias,
etc.*

Orchard Nurseries,
Foston,
Grantham,
Lincolnshire NG32 2LE.
(Tel. 0400 81354)
General nursery

Pennells Nurseries,
Brant Road,
Lincoln LN5 9AF.
(Tel. 0522 820376)
*Clematis and climbers;
garden centres at
Newark Road, Lincoln,
and Humberstone Road,
Cleethorpes*

Potterton & Martin,
The Cottage Nursery,
Moortown Road,
Nettleton,
Caistor,
Lincolnshire LN7 6HX.
(Tel. 0472 851792)
*Alpines, dwarf bulbs,
conifers, shrubs and
carnivorous plants)*

Rectory Cottage,
Wood Enderby,
Horncastle Boston,
Lincolnshire PE22 7PQ.
(Tel. 065 886 252)
Herbaceous perennials

London
Bonsai Kai of London,
c/o 39 West Square,
London SE11 4SP.
Bonsai

British Bonsai
Association,
c/o Flat D,
15 St John's Park,
Blackheath,
London SE3 7TH.
Bonsai

Drysdale Nurseries
(Office),
96 Drysdale Avenue,
Chingford,
London E4 7PE.
(Tel. 01-524 4074)
*Shrubs, conifers and
National Reference
Collection of bamboo*

Kai,
91 St John's Wood
Terrace,
London NW8 6PY.
Bonsai

Longmans Ltd,
16 Holborn Viaduct,
London EC1.
*House and conservatory
plants, royal wedding
bouquets*

Merseyside
Buckels,
Copplehouse Lane,
Fazakerley,
Liverpool L10 0AG.
(Tel. 051 525 2712)
General nursery

Middlesex
Amand, Jacques, Ltd,
Clamphill,
Stanmore,
Middlesex HA7 3JS.
Bulbous plants

Syon Park Garden Centre,
Brentford,
Middlesex TW8 8JF.
(Tel. 01-568 0134)
Unusual plants

Wildwoods Water
Gardens,
Theobalds Park Road,
Crews Hill,
Enfield,
Middlesex EN2 9BP.
(Tel. 01-366 0243/4)
Geraniums,
pelargoniums and
fuchsias

Norfolk
Beales, Peter, Roses,
London Road,
Attleborough,
Norfolk NR17 1AY.
Old-fashioned shrub and
climbing roses

Blooms Nurseries Plc,
Bressingham Gardens,
Diss,
Norfolk IP22 2AB.
(Tel. 0379 88464)
Shrubs, dwarf conifers,
herbaceous plants and
alpines

Bowers, Chris, & Sons,
Whispering Trees
Nursery,
Wimbotsham,
Norfolk PE34 8QB.
Trained fruit trees,
shrubs and herbaceous
plants

Clements, Tony,
African Violet Centre,
Station Road,
Terrington
St Clement,
King's Lynn,
Norfolk PE34 4PL.
Saintpaulias,
streptocarpus and other
Gesneriaceae

Daphne ffiske Herbs,
Rosemary Cottage,
Bramerton,
Norwich,
Norfolk NR14 7DW.
(Tel. 050 88 8187)
Herbs including own
cultivars

Four Seasons,
Hillhouse Farm,
Cheney's Lane,
Forncett St Mary,
Norfolk NR16 1JT.
Herbaceous plants

Hoecroft Plants,
Sheringham Road,
West Beckham,
Holt,
Norfolk NR25 6PQ.
(Tel. 0263 824691)
240 varieties of
variegated and
300 varieties of
coloured-leaved plants in
all species

Norfolk Lavender,
Caley Hill,
Heacham,
King's Lynn,
Norfolk PE31 7JE.
(Tel. 0485 70384)
National Collection of
lavandula

Norwich Heather &
Conifer Centre,
54a Yarmouth Road,
Thorpe,
Norwich,
Norfolk NR14 6PU.
(Tel. 0603 39434)
Conifers and heathers

Old Presbytery Conifer
Gardens,
Stoke Ferry Road,
Oxborough,
King's Lynn,
Norfolk PE33 9PS.
(Tel. 0366 21229)
Over 250 varieties of
conifers and thousands
of heathers

Raveningham
Gardens,
Norwich,
Norfolk NR14 6NS.
Plants noted for foliage,
berries, bark and texture

Van Tubergen UK
Ltd,
Bressingham,
Diss,
Norfolk IP22 2AB.
(Tel. 0379 88 8282)
Tulips, narcissi,
hyacinths and other
spring- and summer-
flowering bulbs

Waveney Fish Farm,
Park Road,
Diss,
Norfolk IP22 3AS.
(Tel. 0379 2697)
Aquatic and marginal
plants

Northamptonshire
Chambers, John,
Wild Flower Seeds,
15 Westleigh Road,
Barton Seagrave,
Kettering,
Northamptonshire
NN15 5AJ.
Wild flowers

Coton Manor Garden,
Nr Ravensthorpe,
Northampton
NN6 8RQ.
(Tel. 0604 740219)
*Herbaceous, foliage
plants and alpines,
especially for clay soils*

Hilltop Alpine Plant
Nursery,
Laxton,
Northamptonshire
NN17 3AX.
(Tel. 078 085 269)
*Alpines; visit advised –
many lines not listed*

Podington Garden
Centre,
High Street,
Podington,
Northamptonshire
NN9 7HS.
General nursery

Spinney Garden,
Grafton Road,
Geddington,
Northamptonshire
NN14 1AJ.
(Tel. 0536 746432)
*Clematis species and
cultivars, wall shrubs,
climbers and herbaceous
plants*

Northumberland
Ashlea Nursery,
Long Framlington,
Morpeth,
Northumberland
NE65 8BB.
(Tel. 066 570 319)
General nursery

Halls of Heddon &
Ovington,
The Nurseries,
Ovington,
Prudhoe,
Northumberland
NE42 6EE.
(Tel. 0661 32467)
*Wide range of both small
and mature herbaceous
and alpine plants*

Herterton House
Nursery,
Hartington,
Cambo,
Morpeth,
Northumberland
NE61 4BN.
(Tel. 067 074 278)
*Country garden plants –
herbaceous, alpine,
ground-cover and
aromatics*

Hexham Herbs,
Chesters Walled Garden,
Chollerford,
Hexham NE48 3AH
(Tel. 0434 681 483)
*National Collection of
thymes, profusion of plants
from bizarre and exotic
locations.*

North Yorkshire
Binks Nurseries Ltd,
Darlington Road,
Northallerton,
North Yorkshire
DL6 2PW.
(Tel. 0609 3992)
*900 varieties of conifers,
herbs and aquatic plants*

Oland Plants,
Sawley Nursery,
Risplith,
Ripon,
North Yorkshire
HG4 3EW.
(Tel. 076 586 622)
*Geraniums, penstemons,
osteospermums, polygonums
and grasses*

Roger, R. V., Ltd,
The Nurseries,
Pickering,
North Yorkshire
YO18 7HG.
(Tel. 0751 72226
*General list of plants
hardy in North of
England*

Stillingfleet Lodge
Nurseries,
Stillingfleet,
North Yorkshire
YO4 6HW.
(Tel. 090 487 506)
*Foliage plants and
unusual perennials;
hardy geraniums,
pulmonarias, variegated
plants and grasses*

Nottinghamshire
Crail Nurseries Ltd,
Newstead Abbey Park,
Nottingham
NE15 8GD.
(Tel. 0623 792866)
Heathers and conifers

Field House Nurseries,
Leake Road,
Gotham,
Nottingham
NG11 0JN.
(Tel. 0602 830278)
General nursery

Humphrey, V. H.,
8 Howbeck Road,
Arnold,
Nottingham
NG5 8AD.
Irises

Laurels Double
Primroses,
46 Maple Drive,
Nuthall,
Nottingham
NG16 1EJ.
*Primroses, mainly
double*

Morton Hall Gardens,
Ranby,
Retford,
Nottingham.
(Tel. 0777 702530)
*Alpines, perennials and
shrubs*

Rosemary Roses,
The Nurseries,
Toton,
Beeston,
Nottingham
NG9 5FH.
Roses

St Helens Croft,
Halam,
Nr Southwell,
Nottinghamshire
NG22 8AY.
(Tel. 0636 813219)
General nursery

Oxfordshire
Castle Alpines,
Castle Road,
Wootton,
Woodstock,
Oxfordshire
OX7 1EG.
(Tel. 0993 812162)
Lime-tolerant alpines

Colegrave Seeds Ltd,
West Adderbury,
Banbury,
Oxfordshire
OX17 3EY.
Annuals grown from seed

Hardy Plant Centre,
Banbury Road,
Chipping Norton,
Oxfordshire OX7 5SY.
(Tel. 0608 41642)
*Irises, geraniums, pinks,
hostas and ferns*

Mattock, John, Ltd,
The Rose Nurseries,
Nuneham Courtenay,
Oxford OX9 9PY.
Roses

Old Inn Cottage Nursery,
Piddington,
Bicester,
Oxfordshire OX6 0PY.
(Tel. 0844 238301)
*Old-fashioned plants,
especially pinks and
auriculas*

Parker-Jervis, J. & E.,
Marten's Hall Farm,
Longworth,
Abingdon,
Oxfordshire
OX13 5EP.
(Tel. 0865 820376
evenings)
*Cottage garden plants
and alpines*

Redman Nurseries,
61 Oxford Road,
Abingdon,
Oxfordshire
OX14 2AA.
(Tel. 0235 20596)
*Wholesale herbaceous
plants; hostas for retail
mail order*

Waterperry
Horticultural Centre,
Nr Wheatley,
Oxfordshire OX9 1JZ.
(Tel. 084 47 226/254)
*General plus National
Reference Collection of
Saxifraga porophylla*

Shropshire
Brynhyfryd Nurseries,
Brynhyfryd,
Rhydycroesau,
Oswestry,
Shropshire SY10.
(Tel. 0691 662725)
*Lewisia and alpines,
conifers and heathers*

Oak Cottage Herb
Farm,
Nesscliffe,
Nr Shrewsbury,
Shropshire SY4 1DB.
(Tel. 074 381 262)
*Herbs, wild flowers, old
roses and cottage plants*

Ridgeway Heather
Nursery,
Horderley Farm,
Horderley,
Nr Craven Arms,
Shropshire SY7 8HP.
(Tel. 058 82 2248)
*Over 100 heathers; also
conifers and acid-loving
shrubs*

Somerset
British Orchid
Council,
Church Bridge Lodge,
Batcombe,
Shepton Mallet,
Somerset BA4 6ER.
Orchids

Broadleigh Gardens,
Bishops Hull,
Taunton,
Somerset TA4 1AE.
*Bulbous and foliage
plants; Californian irises*

Clapton Court
Gardens,
Crewkerne,
Somerset TA18 8PT.
(Tel. 0460 73220/
72200)
*Unusual shrubs, plants
and trees; pelargoniums
and fuchsias*

Dunstan Garden
Design,
Maperton,
Wincanton,
Somerset BA9 8EJ.
(Tel. 0963 32521)
*Astilbes, epimediums,
bergenias, eryngiums,
euphorbias, hostas and
rodgersias*

Durston (Somerset)
Woodlands,
Elmfield,
Higher Durston,
Taunton,
Somerset TA3 5AQ.
(Tel. 0823 412387)
*Shrubs, ornamental and
fruit trees (bare-rooted
and container-grown)*

Fuller, Rodney,
Coachman's Cottage,
Higher Bratton
Seymour,
Wincanton,
Somerset BA9 9BY.
*Violas, violettas, sweet
violets*

Hadspen House
Garden & Nursery,
Castle Cary,
Somerset.
(Tel. 0963 50939/
50200)
General nursery

Kelways Nurseries,
Langport,
Somerset TA10 9SL.
(Tel. 0458 250521)
*Herbaceous plants,
liliums, dahlias*

Kingsfield Tree Nursery,
Broadenham Lane,
Winsham,
Chard,
Somerset TA20 4JF.
(Tel. 0460 30697)
Hardy herbaceous plants.

Mallet Court Nursery,
Curry Mallet,
Taunton,
Somerset TA3 6SY.
(Tel. 0823 480748)
*Maples, oaks and other
rare and unusual plants,
including some from
China and South Korea*

The Margery Fish
Nursery,
East Lambrook Manor,
East Lambrook,
South Petherton,
Somerset.
(Tel. 0460 40328)
*Cranesbills and hardy
geraniums, euphorbias,
hellebores,* Primula
vulgaris

Marston Exotics,
Hurst Lodge,
Martock,
Somerset.
Carnivorous plants

Otters' Court
Heathers,
Otters' Court,
West Camel,
Yeovil,
Somerset BA22 7QF.
(Tel. 0935 850285)
Lime-tolerant heathers

Pilton Manor
Vineyard,
Manor House,
Pilton,
Shepton Mallet,
Somerset BA4 4BE.
(Tel. 074 989 325)
*Vines (wine varieties
only)*

Scotts Nurseries
(Merriott) Ltd,
Merriott,
Somerset TA16 5PL.
(Tel. 0460 72306)
Wide general range.

Sei Yo Kan Bonsai,
Buttercup Cottage,
Corfe,
Nr Taunton,
Somerset TA3 7BY.
Bonsai

West Country Plants,
Maxdene,
South Cary,
Castle Cary,
Somerset.
Herbaceous plants

South Yorkshire
Greenland Vines,
5 Greenland Cottages,
High Hoyland,
Barnsley,
South Yorkshire
S75 4AZ.
(Tel. 0226 385665)
Vines for winemaking

The Heather Garden,
139 Swinston Hill
Road,
Dinnington,
Sheffield,
South Yorkshire
S31 7RY.
(Tel. 0909 565510)
*Heathers, dwarf
conifers, alpines,
potentillas, hebes, roses
and hardy fuchsias*

Hobson, D. T. &
J. A.,
130 Aughton Road,
Swallownest,
Sheffield,
South Yorkshire
S311 0TH
(Tel. 0742 872532)
Fuchsias

Markham Grange
Nurseries,
Long Lands Lane,
Brodsworth,
Nr Doncaster,
South Yorkshire
DN5 7XB.
(Tel. 0302 722390)
Fuchsias

Oscroft's,
Sprotborough Road,
Doncaster,
South Yorkshire
DN5 8BE.
(Tel. 0302 785026)
Dahlias

Walker's Nursery,
Blaxton,
Nr Doncaster,
South Yorkshire
DN9 3BA.
(Tel. 0302 770325)
Wide general range

Staffordshire
Barncroft Nurseries,
Dunwood Lane,
Longsdon,
Stoke-on-Trent,
Staffordshire ST9 9QW.
(Tel. 0538 384310/
372111)
*Very large range of
heathers, conifers and
shrubs*

Bluebell Nursery,
Blackfordby,
Burton-on-Trent,
Staffordshire.
Unusual plants

Conroy Fuchsias,
8 Kingfisher Crescent,
Cheadle,
Stoke-on-Trent,
Staffordshire
ST10 1RZ.
(Tel. 0538 755845)
Fuchsias

Hall Nurseries,
Stretton Road,
Lapley, Staffordshire
ST19 9QQ.
(Tel. 0785 840281)
*Chrysanthemums and
fuchsias*

Jackson's Nurseries,
Clifton Campville,
Nr Tamworth,
Staffordshire B79 0AP.
(Tel. 0827 86 307)
Fuchsias

Suffolk
Barcock, F. G. & Co.,
Garden House Farm,
Drinkstone,
Suffolk IP30 9TN.
(Tel. 044 93 249)
*Trees, shrubs, herbs and
alpines*

Denbeigh Heather
Nurseries,
All Saints Road,
Creeting St Mary,
Ipswich,
Suffolk IP6 8PJ.
(Tel. 0449 711220)
Rooted heather cuttings

Fisk's Clematis
Nursery,
Westleton,
Saxmundham,
Suffolk IP17 3AJ.
(Tel. 072 873 263)
Clematis

Goldbrook Plants,
Hoxne,
Eye,
Suffolk IP21 5AN.
(Tel. 0379 75 770)
*Wide range of shrubs
and hardy plants,
especially foliage, shade
and bog plants*

Home Meadows
Nursery Ltd,
Top Street,
Martlesham
Woodbridge,
Suffolk IP12 4RD.
(Tel. 039 43 2419)
*Bedding plants,
chrysanthemums,
dahlias, hardy plants and
Iceland poppies*

Netherfield Herbs,
Netherfield Cottage,
Nether Street,
Rougham,
Suffolk IP30 9LW.
(Tel. 0359 70452)
*Large range of herbs;
herb garden open daily;
lectures, courses and
design service*

Notcutts Nurseries Ltd,
Woodbridge,
Suffolk IP12 4AF.
(Tel. 039 43 3344)
Wide general nursery

Paradise Centre,
Twinstead Road,
Lamarsh,
Nr Bures,
Suffolk CO8 5EX.
*Bulbous and tuberous
plants*

Rougham Hall Nurseries,
Ipswich Road,
Rougham,
Bury St Edmunds,
Suffolk IP30 9LZ.
(Tel. 0359 70577/
70153)
*Iceland poppies and
other spring-flowering
perennials; named
varieties of delphinium*

Surrey
Badshot Lea Garden
Centre,
Badshot Lea Road,
Farnham,
Surrey GU9 9JK.
(Tel. 0252 333666)
Herbaceous perennials

Bowlby, Rupert,
Gatton,
Reigate,
Surrey RH2 0TA.
*Spring- and summer-
flowering bulbous plants*

British and European
Geranium Society,
c/o 85 Sparrow Farm Road,
Ewell,
Surrey KT37 2LP.
*Regal and zonal
pelargoniums*

Bromage and Young
Ltd,
St Mary's Gardens,
Worplesdon,
Surrey GU3 3RS.
Bonsai

Chessington Nurseries
Ltd,
Leatherhead Road,
Chessington,
Surrey.
Houseplants

Cuddington Nursery,
Cuddington Way,
Cheam,
Surrey SM2 7JB.
*Geraniums,
pelargoniums and
fuchsias*

Green Farm Plants,
Bentley,
Farnham,
Surrey GU10 5JX.
(Tel. 0420 23202)
*Small shrubs, alpines,
sub-shrubs and
perennials, many
uncommon*

The Hardy Plant
Society,
21 Ruxley Lane,
West Ewell,
Surrey KT17 9EU.
*Dicentras,
polygonatums, bergenias
and other hardy
herbaceous plants*

Herons Bonsai Nursery
Ltd,
Wiremill Lane,
Newchapel,
Nr Lingfield,
Surrey RH7 6HJ.
Bonsai

High Trees Nurseries,
Buckland,
Reigate,
Surrey RH2 9RE.
(Tel. 073 72 47271)
*Fuchsias, geraniums,
bedding plants, alpines,
heathers, trees, shrubs
and roses*

Hydon Nurseries Ltd,
Clock Barn Lane,
Hydon Heath,
Godalming,
Surrey GU8 4AZ.
*Rhododendrons, azaleas,
enkianthus, pieris and
hostas*

Knaphill Nursery Ltd,
Barrs Lane,
Lower Knaphill,
Woking,
Surrey GU21 2JW.
*Rhododendrons, azaleas
and associated plants*

Millais Nurseries,
Crosswater Farm,
Churt,
Farnham,
Surrey GU10 2JN.
(Tel. 025 125 2415)
*Rhododendrons and
azaleas*

Nettletons Nursery,
Ivy Mill Lane,
Godstone,
Surrey RH9 8NH.
(Tel. 0883 842426)
*Trees and shrubs,
especially conifers,
azaleas, camellias,
rhododendrons; vines
and climbers*

Peters Gardens,
Stoke Road,
Stoke D'Abernon,
Cobham,
Surrey KT11 3PU.
(Tel. 0932 62530)
*Herbaceous plants, shrubs,
alpines and water plants*

Russell, L. R., Ltd,
Richmond Nurseries,
Windlesham,
Surrey GU20 6LL.
(Tel. 0990 21411/2)
Shrubs and perennials

Sunningdale Nurseries Ltd,
London Road,
Windlesham,
Surrey GU20 6LN.
(Tel. 0990 23166)
Very wide general range

Wisley Plant Centre,
Nr Ripley,
Woking,
Surrey GU23 6QB.
(Tel. 0483 224234)
*Herbaceous plants, shrubs,
fruit, bulbs and tropical plants*

Warwickshire
Court Farm Nursery,
Honeybourne Road,
Pebworth,
Nr Stratford-upon-
Avon,
Warwickshire
CV37 8XP.
Hellebores

Fibrex Nurseries Ltd,
Honeybourne Road,
Pebworth,
Stratford-upon-Avon,
Warwickshire
CV37 8XT.
(Tel. 0789 720788)
Ivies and ferns

The John Beach
Clematis Nursery,
Thelsford Farm,
Charlecote,
Warwickshire.
(Tel. 0926 624173)
Clematis

Woodfield Bros,
71 Townsend Road,
Tiddington,
Stratford-upon-Avon,
Warwickshire
CV37 7DF.
Hybrid lupins

West Midlands
Cypress Nursery
Powke Lane,
Blackheath,
Birmingham,
West Midlands
B65 0AG.
(Tel. 021 559 1495)
*Geranium hybridisers,
trees, shrubs, heathers,
alpines and herbaceous
plants*

H. Woolman
(Dorridge) Ltd,
Grange Road,
Dorridge,
Solihull,
West Midlands
B93 8QB.
*Chrysanthemums,
pelargoniums and fuchsias*

West Sussex
Allwood Bros,
Mill Nursery,
Hassocks,
West Sussex BN6 9NB.
*Carnations, pinks and
venidio-arctotis*

Dahlia Haven Plants,
28 Hillside,
Horsham,
West Sussex RH12 1NG.
(Tel. 0403 67792)
*Dahlias and
chrysanthemums*

Holly Gate Cactus
Nursery,
Ashington,
West Sussex RH20 3BA.
*Cacti, succulents and
xerophytes*

Ingwersen,
W. E. Th., Ltd,
Birch Farm Nursery,
Gravetye,
East Grinstead,
West Sussex RH19 4LE.
*Alpine plants, dwarf
shrubs and bulbs*

Leonardslee Gardens,
Lower Beeding,
Nr Horsham,
West Sussex
RH13 6PP.
(Tel. 040 376 412)
*Rhododendrons and
azaleas in all sizes*

Mitchell, Mary &
Peter,
11 Wingle Tye Road,
Burgess Hill,
West Sussex RH15 9HR.
(Tel. 044 46 6848)
*Sempervivums,
jovibarbas, rosularias*

Nightingale Garden
Centre,
14 Nightingale Road,
Horsham,
West Sussex.
(Tel. 0403 55155)
General nursery

Smith, P. J.,
Chanctonbury
Nursery,
Rectory Lane,
Ashington,
West Sussex RH20 3AS.
Hybrid alstroemerias,
bouvardias and
gypsophilas

Stonehurst Nurseries,
Ardingly,
Haywards Heath,
West Sussex RH17 6TN.
(Tel. 0444 892436)
Camellias, shrubs and
conifers

Vesutor Ltd,
Marringdean Road,
Billingshurst,
West Sussex
RH14 9EH.
Bromeliads

Wickenden, M. C.,
Well Meadow,
Crawley Down,
West Sussex R10 4EY.
Unusual perennials;
agapanthus, crocosmias,
erodiums, eryngiums,
euphorbias, geraniums,
etc.

West Yorkshire
Craven, S. R. & M.,
Antique Auriculas,
1 Foulds Terrace,
Bingley,
West Yorkshire
BD16 4LZ.
(Tel. 0274 561412)
Show auriculas,
primulas, pinks, alpines
and specialist seeds

Waincliffe Garden
Nursery,
24 Bradford Road,
Northowram,
Halifax,
West Yorkshire
HX3 7HH.
(Tel. 0422 202639)
Ericaceous plants, mainly
rhododendrons; also saxifrages
and primulas

Wiltshire
Avon Bulbs,
Westwood,
Bradford-on-Avon,
Wiltshire BA15 2AT.
Bulbous plants

Bowood Garden Centre,
Bowood Estate,
Calne,
Wiltshire.
(Tel. 0249 816828)
Wide range of shrubs,
trees, rhododendrons,
many rare and unusual

Harley, W. & L.,
Parham Nursery,
The Sands,
Market Lavington,
Wiltshire SN10 4QA.
(Tel. 038 081 3712)
Wide range of alpines and
perennials in traditional and
unusual varieties

Manningford
Nurseries,
Manningford Abbots,
Nr Pewsey,
Wiltshire SN9 5PB.
(Tel. 0672 62232)
Specialists in 18th and
19th century plants,
particularly cottage
garden types

Startley Hill Nurseries,
Startley,
Chippenham,
Wiltshire SN15 5HQ.
(Tel. 0249 720674)
Herbaceous perennials

Westfield Plants,
Great Chalfield,
Melksham,
Wiltshire SN12 8NN.
Rare hardy shrubs and
perennials

WALES

Clwyd
Aberconwy Nursery,
Graig,
Glan Conwy,
Clwyd LL28 7TL.
(Tel. 049 268 875)
Astilbes and penstemons

Bodnant Garden
Nursery,
Tal-y-Cafn,
Colwyn Bay,
Clwyd LL28 5RE.
(Tel. 049 267 460)
Rhododendrons,
camellias and magnolias;
wide range of unusual
trees and shrubs

Dyfed
Manorbier Garden
Centre,
Manorbier,
Tenby,
Dyfed SA70 7SG.
(Tel. 0834 82206)
Lime-tolerant species

St Ishmael's Nursery
and Garden Centre,
St Ishmael's,
Haverfordwest,
Dyfed SA62 3SY.
(Tel. 064 65 343)
General nursery

Tyn-y-Ffordd Nursery,
Ponterwyd,
Aberystwyth,
Dyfed SY23 3JR.
(Tel. 097 085 662)
General nursery

Gwent
Yew Tree Nursery,
Lydart,
Monmouth,
Gwent.
(Tel. 0600 2293)
General nursery

Gwynedd
The Herb Garden,
Cae-Rhos-Lligwy,
Brynteg,
Anglesey,
Gwynedd.
(Tel. 0248 853407)
Herbs

Powys
Dyfi Bridge Garden
Centre,
Machynlleth,
Powys SY20 8BL.
(Tel. 0654 2086)
Old roses and herbs

SCOTLAND

Central Region
Blairhoyle Nursery,
Port of Monteith,
Stirlingshire,
Central Region
FK8 3LF.
(Tel. 08775 669)
*Heathers, alpines and
dwarf conifers*

**Dumfries and
Galloway**
Beeswing Nursery,
Beeswing,
Dumfries and
Galloway DG2 8PE.
(Tel. 038 776 232)
Rhododendrons

Cally Gardens,
Gatehouse of Fleet,
Castle Douglas,
Dumfries and
Galloway DG7 2DJ.
Rare herbaceous plants

King & Paton,
Barnhourie Mill,
By Dalbeattie,
Dumfries and
Galloway DG5 4PU.
(Tel. 038 778 269)
Rhododendrons

Fife
Pennyacre Nurseries,
Station Road,
Springfield,
Fife KY15 5RU.
(Tel. 0334 55852)
*Heathers and dwarf
conifers*

Grampian
Chalmers, David W.,
West Blackbutts,
Stonehaven,
Grampian AB3 2RT.
(Tel. 0569 30430)
*Dwarf hardy primulas,
double primroses,
hepaticas, bellis and
violas*

Reid, Ben & Co.,
Pinewood Park,
Countesswells Road,
Aberdeen,
Grampian AB9 2QL.
(Tel. 0224 38744)
Trees and shrubs

Trellis Nursery,
Durris,
Banchory,
Grampian AB3 3BD.
(Tel. 033 08 397)
*Ground-cover and water
plants, gentians,
geraniums*

Highland Region
Abriachan Nurseries,
Loch Ness Side,
Inverness IV3 6LA.
(Tel. 046 386 232)
*Alpines, herbs and hardy
border plants*

Drake, Jack,
Inshriach Alpine
Nursery,
Aviemore,
Inverness PH22 1QS.
(Tel. 054 04 287)
*Rare and unusual
alpines and rock plants,
especially primulas,
meconopsis, gentians,
heathers*

Highland Liliums,
Kiltarlity-by-Beauly,
Inverness IV4 7JQ.
(Tel. 046 374 365)
Herbaceous plants,
alpines and liliums

Munro, Iris,
Elrig,
Cantray,
Croy,
Inverness.
Pelargoniums

Poyntzfield Herb Nursery,
Black Isle,
By Dingwall,
Ross-shire IV7 8LX.
(Tel. 038 18 352
evenings)
Over 300 popular,
unusual and rare herbs

Riverbank Nursery
Centre,
Riverbank Road,
Conon Bridge,
Dingwall,
Ross-shire IV7 8BT.
(Tel. 0349 61720)
General nursery

Speyside Heather
Garden Centre,
Dulnain Bridge,
Highland Region
PH26 3PA.
(Tel. 047 985 359)
Heathers and alpines,
conifers, shrubs

Lothian
Plants from the Past,
The Old House,
1 North Street,
Belhaven,
Dunbar,
Lothian EH42 1NU.
(Tel. 0368 63223)
Aquilegias, artemisias,
bellis, campanulas,
dianthus, erysimums,
hederas, helichrysums

Edrom Nurseries,
Coldingham,
Eyemouth,
Berwick-upon-Tweed,
TD14 5TZ.
(Tel. 089 07 71386)
Primulas, gentians,
meconopsis, anemones
and other alpines

Strathclyde
Barguillean Nurseries Ltd,
Taynuilt,
Strathclyde PA35 1Y.
(Tel. 086 62 333)
Herbaceous and
ericaceous plants

Kinlochlaich House,
Garden Plant Centre,
Appin,
Strathclyde
PA38 43D.
(Tel. 063 173 342)
Plants to suit local mild,
moist conditions

Tayside
Angus Heathers,
10 Guthrie Street,
Letham,
Forfar,
Tayside DD8 2PS.
(Tel. 030 781 504)
Heathers and gentians

Bonhard Nursery,
Murrayshall Road,
Scone,
Tayside.
(Tel. 0738 52791)
Woodland plants

Glendoick Gardens Ltd,
Glencarse,
Perth PN2 7NS.
(Tel. 073 886 205)
Rhododendrons, azaleas
and ericaceous plants;
National Collection of
kalmia

Glenview Alpine
Nursery,
Quarryhill,
By Forfar,
Angus,
Tayside DD8 3TQ.
(Tel. 030 786 205)
Alpines

Laurie, James, & Sons,
Blackness Nursery,
Ninewells,
Dundee DD2 1PX.
(Tel. 0382 68360)
Unusual plants

NORTHERN IRELAND

County Down
Daisy Hill Nurseries Ltd,
Hospital Road,
Newry,
County Down
BT35 8PN.
(Tel. 0693 2474)
Wide variety of trees and
shrubs, especially
camellia, ceanothus;
herbaceous plants,
alpines and heathers

◆ GARDENING ◆ FOR THE ELDERLY AND DISABLED

There are many books, special gardening equipment and organisations that can be of help to those who, through illness, accident or old age, find they are less able to cope with a garden.

◆ BOOKS AND OTHER PUBLICATIONS ◆

Gardening Equipment for the Disabled, David Hollinrake (£6.00 inc. p&p)
Available from:
Equipment for the Disabled,
Mary Marlborough Lodge,
Nuffield Orthopaedic Centre,
Headington,
Oxford OX3 7LD.

Gardening Without Sight, Kathleen Fleet (send SAE for up to five free copies)
Available from:
Royal National Institute for the Blind,
224 Great Portland Street,
London WLN 6AA.

Gardening in Retirement, Isobel Pays (£1.95 inc. p&p)
Contains ideas for existing gardens and practical advice for people who are not so young. Available from:
Publications Department,
Age Concern England,
Bernard Sunley House,
60 Pitcairn Road,
Mitcham,
Surrey CR4 3LL.

The Low Maintenance Garden, Graham Rose (£10.95 inc. p&p)
An illustrated guide with ideas for creating a garden that looks after itself.
Available from most bookshops, but if difficult to obtain, contact:

Frances Lincoln Ltd,
Apollo Works,
5 Charlton Kings Road,
London NW5 2SB.

Gardening is for Everyone, A. Cloes and C. Underhill (£6.95 hardback;
£4.95 paperback)
A week-by-week illustrated ideas guide for people with handicaps showing
that even those with limited mobility can create a beautiful garden of their
own. Available at most bookshops, but if difficult to obtain, contact:
Souvenir Press,
43 Great Russell Street,
London WC1B 3PA.

Easy-to-make Aids for Elderly People, Don Caston (£8.95 hardback; £5.95
paperback)
An imaginative and practical illustrated book with more than a hundred
ideas for cheap and easy-to-make aids and adaptations to ensure an easier
life in and around the home. Available from most bookshops or from
Souvenir Press at the address above.

Gardens for Physically Disabled Gardeners (80p inc. p&p)
Send a postal order or cheque to:
Capel Manor Horticultural & Environmental Centre,
Bullsmore Lane,
Enfield,
Middlesex EN1 4RQ.
Capel Manor has also produced a video, *Countryside Recreation for the
Disabled*, concerning ways of improving access to countryside for disabled
people. This costs £49.00 + VAT, or may be rented weekly at
£13.30 + VAT.

Keep on Gardening (£1.25 inc. p&p)
A Herefordshire guide for disabled and elderly gardeners describing how to
'keep on growing', with suggestions for the design of and information
about tools, books and organisations. Available from:
DIAL,
15 St Owen Street,
Hereford HR1 2JB.

Gardening for People with Disabilities, G. Mostert (£1.20 inc. p&p)
Ideas for disabled gardening simply and practically outlined. Available from:
Gardens for the Disabled Trust,
Old House Farm,
Peasmarsh,
East Sussex TN31 6YD.

The Garden and the Handicapped Child, P. Elliott (£3.95 inc. p&p)
For all those involved in caring for children, containing ideas for
gardening technique and practice. Available from:
Haigh & Hochland Ltd,
The Precinct Centre,
Oxford Road,
Manchester M13 9QA.

Growth Point – Horticultural Therapy
A quarterly magazine for gardeners with special needs. Annual
subscription: £10.00
Horticultural Therapy also has a large selection of leaflets from 40p on
everything from tools to techiques and design. For the magazine and a
comprehensive list of leaflets, send an SAE to:
Growth Point,
Horticultural Therapy,
Goulds Ground,
Vallis Way,
Frome,
Somerset BA11 3DW.

The *Horticultural Group* of the University of Bath offers a series of
publications on horticulture and landscape provision for people who are
elderly and/or have disabilities. A list is available from:
Peter Thoday,
Horticultural Group,
School of Biological Sciences,
University of Bath,
Claverton Down,
Bath BA2 7AY.

♦ USEFUL ORGANISATIONS ♦

Horticultural Therapy,
Goulds Ground,
Vallis Way,
Frome,
Somerset BA11 3DW.
(Tel. 0373 64782)
Aims to 'enrich the lives of people who are disabled, and of others seeking
support in using gardens as a therapy'. Offers training, advice, volunteers,
demonstration gardens, workshop service. See also under 'Books and
Other Publications', page 152.

Gardens for the Disabled Trust,
c/o The Honorary Secretary,
Old House Farm,
Peasmarsh,
East Sussex TN31 6YD.
Runs a garden club which gives free advice and financial help to enable
people with any disability to take an active part in gardening.

South Regional Association for the Blind/The Advisory Committee for
Blind Gardeners,
c/o 55 Eton Avenue,
Swiss Cottage,
London NW3 3ET.
(Tel. 01-722 9703)
Fosters among people who are visually impaired an interest in gardening in
all its forms. Information on a variety of subjects is available.

Buckinghamshire Association for Gardening with Disabled People,
c/o George C. Ward,
Lane Cottage,
Church Lane,
Lacey Green,
Aylesbury HP17 0QX.
(Tel. 084 44 5075)

Yorkshire Association for Gardening with Disabled People,
c/o Philip Ruston,
Spofforth Hall Cheshire Home,
Nr Harrogate HG3 1BX.
(Tel. 093 782 284)
These two associations actively help people with disabilities, who are
living at home, to garden themselves.

Federation to Promote Horticulture for Disabled People,
c/o Monica Rhodes,
9 Miles Close,
Yapton,
Arundel,
West Sussex BN18 0TB.
(Tel. 0903 724014)
A national organisation which assists, in a variety of ways, gardeners who
are disabled.

Growth Unlimited,
Voluntary Action Camden,
Instrument House,
207–215 Kings Cross Road,
London WC1X 9DB.
(Tel. 01-388 2071)
Encourages the practical involvement of people with disabilities in
horticultural activities within the London Borough of Camden.

Special Interest Group for Remedial Gardening (SPRIG),
c/o John Catlin,
252 The Ridgeway,
Enfield,
Middlesex EN2 8AP.
SPRIG provides a focus for professionals working within the NHS to
promote horticultural therapy for people with any disability.

For information about public gardens with access for disabled people or
demonstration gardens, contact:

National Trust,
36 Queen Anne's Gate,
London SW1H 9AS.
(Tel. 01-222 9251)
The NT publishes a leaflet, *Facilities for Disabled and Visually Handicapped
Visitors*, available from the above address (please send an SAE).

National Trust for Scotland,
5 Charlotte Square,
Edinburgh EH2 4DU.
(Tel. 031 226 5922)
The NT for Scotland publishes a leaflet, *Information about Trust Properties
for Disabled Visitors*, available from the above address (please send an
SAE).

◆ ORGANIC PRODUCTS ◆

ORGANIC PESTICIDES

Name of Product	Pest Controlled
Aeroxon Flying Insect Trap	Greenhouse pests
Derris Dust	Caterpillars, aphids and other pests
Derris-Pyrethrum Spray	Most insect pests. Can be harmful to bees and ladybirds, so use sparingly in the evenings. Non-toxic to humans and pets
Quassia Chips	Aphids
Phostrogen Safer's Insecticidal Soap	Aphids, whitefly, mealy bugs
Phostrogen Safer's Natural Garden Fungicide	Black spot, powdery mildew and scab

BIOLOGICAL PEST CONTROL

Name of Control	Description
Whitefly control (*Encarsia formosa*)	A tiny parasitic wasp that lays its eggs in the whitefly larva
Red spider mite control (*Phytoseilus persimilis*)	A predator of red spider mite
Bactospeine WP (*Bacillus thuringiensis*)	Specific to certain caterpillars. Will not harm anything else
Trappit codling moth trap	Synthetic pheromone attracts male codling moths to stick trap
Cryptolaemus monttrouzieri	Predator of mealy bug

WIDELY AVAILABLE ORGANIC FERTILISERS

Name of Product	Main Active Ingredient
Bonemeal	Phosphate
Blood, fish and bonemeal	Phosphate and nitrogen
Hoof and horn	Nitrogen
Rock phosphate	
Rock potash	Potassium
Seaweed meal	Nitrogen and potassium

SUPPLIERS OF BIOLOGICAL PEST CONTROL PRODUCTS

Bunting & Sons,
The Nurseries,
Great Horkesley,
Colchester,
Essex CM6 4AJ.
(Tel. 0206 271300)
Encarsia, Phytoseilus, Cryptolaemus

English Woodland Ltd,
Hoyle Depot,
Graffham,
Petworth,
West Sussex GU28 0LR.
(Tel. 079 86 574)
Encarsia, Phytoseilus, Cryptolaemus

Natural Pest Control,
Watermead,
Yapton Road,
Barnham,

Bognor Regis,
West Sussex PO22 0BQ.
Encarsia, Phytoseilus, Cryptolaemus

Steele & Brodie (1983) Ltd,
Stevens Drove,
Houghton,
Stockbridge,
Hampshire SO20 6LP.
Trappit

Henry Doubleday Research
Association, National Centre
for Organic Gardening,
Ryton-on-Dunsmore,
Coventry CV8 3LG.
(Tel. 0203 303517)
Most organic products and advice

GARDENS TO VISIT

Have you ever been told by a friend that there is a marvellous garden at so and so and that you really must go and see? Then, having driven umpteen miles, you are welcomed by a sign on the gate saying 'Closed'? You can avoid all frustrations and have a list of numerous gardens in every county – when they open, what they charge, whether they serve teas and so on – by buying the following magic books:

Gardens of England and Wales
Send £2.25 (which includes postage) to:
The National Gardens Scheme
Charitable Trust,
Hatchlands Park,
East Clandon,
Guildford,
Surrey GU4 7RT
(Tel. 0483 211535)

Gardens of Scotland
Send £2.00 (which includes postage) to:
Scotland's Gardens Scheme,
31 Castle Terrace,
Edinburgh EH1 2EL
(Tel. 031 229 1870)

If you think your garden is worthy of inclusion, and you would like to open it to the public two or three times a year for charity, write to the appropriate organisation at the address given above.

◆ INDEX ◆